Essential Law for Counsellors and Psychotherapists

Legal Resources for Counsellors and Psychotherapists

Legal Resources for Counsellors and Psychotherapists is a series of highly practical books, themed around broad topics, which reflect the most 'frequently asked questions' put to the BACP's professional advice line.

Books in the series:

Therapists in Court: Providing Evidence and Supporting Witnesses
Tim Bond and Amanpreet Sandhu

Confidentiality and Record Keeping in Counselling and Psychotherapy
Tim Bond and Barbara Mitchels

Essential Law for Counsellors and Psychotherapists

3

bacp

British Association for
Counselling & Psychotherapy

Barbara Mitchels and Tim Bond

Los Angeles | London | New Delhi
Singapore | Washington DC

First published 2010

SAGE Publications Ltd
1 Oliver's Yard
55 City Road
London EC1Y 1SP

SAGE Publications Inc.
2455 Teller Road
Thousand Oaks, California 91320

SAGE Publications India Pvt Ltd
B 1/I 1 Mohan Cooperative Industrial Area
Mathura Road
New Delhi 110 044

SAGE Publications Asia-Pacific Pte Ltd
3 Church Street
#10-04 Samsung Hub
Singapore 049483

Library of Congress Control Number: 2009938667

British Library Cataloguing in Publication data

A catalogue record for this book is available from
the British Library

ISBN 978-1-84860-885-6
ISBN 978-1-84860-886-3 (pbk)

Typeset by C&M Digitals (P) Ltd, Chennai, India
Printed and bound in Great Britain by Ashford Colour Press Ltd.
Printed on paper from sustainable resources

Contents

List of Checklists, Figures and Tables

Acknowledgements

We are indebted to all the lawyers, academics, insurance advisers and others who have assisted in providing information and resources for this book. It covers such a wide range of law and practice that we have really appreciated the ideas drawn from the collective experience of practitioners in the fields which we have addressed. In particular we thank Helen M. Watts, Advocate, for her contributions to the book on the law in Scotland. We would also like to express our especial gratitude to solicitors Rodney Nelson Jones and Philip Hook for reading through parts of the manuscript with a critical eye.

We are also grateful to the many therapists from different backgrounds and settings who have shared their experience of how the law has helped or hindered them and all those who have discussed legal issues with us. There is no way of naming everyone individually but we hope that they will recognise some of their concerns addressed in this book.

Trying to find the answers to some of the legal questions that have been posed to us has been challenging, and in particular we thank publishers Taylor & Francis, LexisNexis and Jordan publishing, who provided us with books and resources for legal research. In relation to insurance, we thank all who helped us, and in particular we thank Towergate and also Steve Johnson and Jo Mountain of Howdens for providing us with information and opportunities for discussion.

Above all we are grateful to the expertise of the staff of BACP, especially to Grainne Griffin and John O'Dowd from the Professional Conduct Department, and Denise Chaytor, Kathleen Daymond and Wendy Brewer, who, with other members of the Information Services Team, drew on their experience of answering members' queries to inform us about many of the issues that they felt needed to be addressed in this book.

Finally we want to express our appreciation to BACP, which has sponsored and supported the writing of this book throughout its creation. The ultimate responsibility for its content rests with us as the authors.

Barbara Mitchels and Tim Bond

Introduction

Therapists have to work within the framework of national and local law in the same way that any other citizen is required to obey the law. This includes both criminal and civil provisions. Criminal law includes offences against the state, individuals, animals or property, for which some form of punishment may be appropriate. Civil law addresses the rights of citizens and regulates relationships between citizens. Law passed by Parliament or created by the courts can be regarded as authoritative or 'hard' law that can be straightforwardly enforced through the courts. The law applies to all counsellors and psychotherapists and to all the aspects of our work. In order to practise within the law, we need to be aware of what it is and how it works.

However, the work of most therapists will also bring them into contact with 'soft' law, such as codes of practice issued by government departments, recommendations from official reports and protocols adopted by statutory services. This type of 'soft law' frequently has no legal status in the courts, in the sense that courts are not obliged to follow it until such time as Parliament gives it full legal status. As we will see later in this book, there are many issues that impact on how therapists work which involve both 'hard' and 'soft' law. Nowhere is this more evident than in government guidance and procedures for the protection of children and vulnerable adults. In order to work professionally, a therapist needs to be able to distinguish between those issues where the scope for professional judgement is curtailed by legal obligation and situations where it is possible to use professional judgement. Frequently, the 'soft law' will be followed by therapists because it is relevant and considered the best way of delivering a service or acting in the interests of a client. Courts have also taken the view that even where 'soft law' is not legally enforceable, they should encourage adherence to it, particularly with regard to child protection. Some 'soft' law may in effect become a legal requirement for the therapist because of the way it is incorporated within the contract of employment (see Chapters 4 and 9). The difference between 'hard' and 'soft' law is only one of the distinctions in the use of law that is considered within this book.

The law can be complex and is divided into different subjects or themes. As a consequence, a single act by a therapist may involve several different aspects of law. For example, imagine the situation of a therapist who makes a disclosure to social services about her fears concerning an adolescent child client (without the client's consent) and then later that day, is assaulted on the counselling premises by the aggrieved father of that client, who breaks a window and damages furniture in the process. That therapist may find themselves giving evidence as a witness in a criminal prosecution of the father for assault and criminal damage. Also, the counsellor may be called as a witness in civil care proceedings concerning the child. In addition, there may be issues about insurance of the counselling premises, and possibly an ethical and contractual issue between the therapist and the client about confidentiality and the appropriate way to disclose information involving both 'hard' and 'soft' law.

As can be seen from the example above, the legal system operates at many levels, and applying the law to any situation is rather like trying to piece together a multidimensional jigsaw puzzle. This book explores various aspects of the law as it might apply to therapists, explaining how (and why) the different areas of law interlink with each other, using examples of different situations encountered from therapeutic practice.

Chapter 1 describes the legal framework in England, Wales and Northern Ireland, the structure of the court system with avenues of appeal, and Chapter 5 considers various aspects of criminal activity.

Chapter 2 looks at public interest and professional standards in law and ethics. Chapter 3 further addresses the need to maintain professional standards and responsibility to clients, considering the acts or omissions that might constitute professional negligence.

Some therapists are self-employed, others are employed or volunteers in agencies, but each of us has to contract in one way or another with clients and with other providers of goods and services, and Chapter 4 deals with the making of contracts, unfair contractual requirements and remedies for breach, while Chapters 8 and 9 look specifically at the therapist as employer/employee.

We have a responsibility to consider public health and safety requirements in relation to our place of work, and to consider our needs and those of our clients in ensuring insurance cover for professional liability and legal responsibility for our work. Chapter 6 looks at how therapists can protect themselves and clients from various types of loss with adequate insurance cover: for example, material things including personal belongings, office equipment and furniture. Chapter 7 explores issues relating to premises, including the law that is relevant to the creation of a safe physical space in which to work with clients, and which needs to be appropriately equipped and properly insured.

Therapists may be involved in a wide variety of legal claims and proceedings. In Chapter 10, we demystify some of the legal jargon and provide resources and links to find the necessary information about making and responding to civil claims, for example, debt collection, county court actions and other civil proceedings. We explain criminal procedure, and help therapists to find their way through the legal maze, including confidentiality and information sharing.

In Chapter 11, we bring the book together by considering the concept of professional diligence and what it means for therapists to act in accordance with the 'hard law' as well as the 'soft law' of government and professional guidance.

In addition, we have to work within the framework of the law in relation to the protection of children and vulnerable adults. In Chapter 5, we include an overview of the new vetting and barring procedures created in England, Wales and Northern Ireland by the Safeguarding Vulnerable Groups Act 2006, which will be implemented incrementally, commencing from 12 October 2009. We also provide resources for information about the new Protection of Vulnerable Groups (Scotland) Act 2007 and its implementation.

Some people have expressed concern that in writing about the law in relation to therapy, we might be somehow 'talking up' legal claims, but we believe that the converse is true. If therapists are reasonably aware of the relevant law and work within it, they might, perhaps, avoid some of the pitfalls and fewer claims may be made.

These areas of law are complex. Knowing that a book of this size cannot address all the issues relevant to each topic (and that therapists do not necessarily want to become lawyers), we have done our best to create a map of the law in relation to therapeutic practice, showing the main legal provisions which might apply, and indicating various ways through the thickets of the law, pointing out along the way where 'there be dragons'. In this way, we hope that this book will help readers to gain confidence in the legal aspects of their work.

However, no book is an adequate substitute for seeking legal advice from an appropriately qualified and experienced lawyer when faced with a legal dilemma or with a court case, claim or complaint. Each therapeutic alliance is different and the law has to be applied to each specific situation. In such circumstances, it is best to seek expert advice from a person qualified in that field and, where appropriate, to notify the professional insurers, who may provide or fund legal assistance. At the back of the book we have provided a list of useful resources.

We refer in the book to '*therapists*', intending to include counsellors and psychotherapists of all approaches and modalities. 'Therapists' also includes closely related roles such as providing coaching, mentoring, consultative support or supervision within a therapeutic context. Where we use 'he' or 'she', we intend these terms to include both genders, unless we say otherwise.

A note on jurisdiction: this book covers the law in England, and the law in Wales and Northern Ireland is covered where specifically mentioned. We have, in certain places, included the law and links to resources in Scotland.

1 Law and Ethics

It would not be correct to say that every moral obligation involves a legal duty; but every legal duty is founded on a moral obligation.

Lord Chief Justice Coleridge in R v Instan [1893] 1 QB at 453
(in Mason and Laurie 2006)

In the Introduction, there was a glimpse of how one situation can give rise to a wide variety of rights, duties and legal actions in both criminal and civil law. This chapter explores how some of the different areas of law relate to each other. We also explore the legal system in England and Wales in 1.2 below. This book covers Northern Ireland, Scotland and other jurisdictions where specifically stated.

As an illustration, imagine an alleged breach of confidentiality where a therapist working in an Employee Assistance Service accidentally addresses a letter about a client to the wrong person. The letter contains sensitive information relevant to the client's credibility and reputation as an employee. This mistake could put the therapist in breach of contract with a client (and her employer) and be the basis of multiple civil wrongs, including breach of her duty of care. Suppose, then, that the therapist, by now very frightened at the potential consequences of her actions, goes further and, when accused of these civil wrongs, offers a fabricated defence that the letter had been stolen and then maliciously addressed by a person (whom she names as the thief) to cause maximum harm. Suppose the therapist also removes documents from her employer's files to hide traces of her own actions. Suddenly we are in the realms of slander, and the criminal offence of theft of the documents and possibly also attempting to pervert the course of justice. Each single action (or a sequence of closely related actions) may create liability in different areas of law and each will have its own specific court, rules of evidence, and type of hearing. The evidence in any civil action may also be used in any criminal prosecution that might be brought, and the evidence of conviction from a criminal hearing might be used in evidence in a civil matter. Evidence from either or both might be used in any subsequent disciplinary hearings by professional bodies.

Understanding the difference between criminal and civil law is fundamental to understanding the application of law to the work of therapists. It determines which courts may be involved with their different rules and approach to evidence. We will return to this topic later. However, we will start with the most basic of questions about what is the relationship between law and ethics. This introductory chapter provides a context for the remainder of the book.

1.1 Law and ethics – relationships and differences

It is often difficult to know what is right. Moral evaluation is both collective and personal, and may be based on a vast eclectic mix which includes social, cultural, religious and family values. Ethics are the result of more systematically considered approaches to distinguishing what is right from wrong. Most professions have developed their own ethical statements as a way of explaining how their work is best undertaken to achieve the greatest good and minimise any potential harms or wrongs. These statements of ethics help professionals to consider the justification for the ways they approach their work.

For example, the *Ethical Framework for Good Practice in Counselling and Psychotherapy* (BACP 2010) (the *Ethical Framework*) sets out shared values across the area of professional activity and provides guidance for conduct and best practice. See also the guidance provided by other associations including, for example, the British Psychological Society (BPS), the United Kingdom Council for Psychotherapy (UKCP), the Confederation of Scottish Counselling Agencies (COSCA) and the government programme, Improving Access to Psychological Therapies (IAPT).

Ethical frameworks are not law, and nor are they, in themselves, legally binding. However, as an expression of the shared values of the profession, they will carry weight within the profession to which they apply, for example, in the consideration of complaints and within disciplinary hearings. Courts may refer to ethical frameworks and to the codes of professional bodies in order to determine what that body has adopted as a reasonable standard of practice. As a result, professional frameworks or codes may have persuasive authority in court cases but no court is bound to follow their requirements.

The law is the system of rules by which international relationships, nations and populations are governed. Law reflects society's prevailing moral values and beliefs, enforcing compliance in various ways, such as fines or imprisonment. It constantly changes and develops along with changes in society. For example, the legislation concerning corporal punishment, homosexuality, child protection, ownership of family property and smoking in public has changed radically over the years.

There are three legal national jurisdictions comprising the United Kingdom (UK), i.e. England and Wales, Northern Ireland and Scotland. Eire (Southern Ireland) is a wholly separate nation state but has many legal features in common with the UK legal system. Similarly, the Isle of Man and the Channel Islands each have their own law-making powers independently of the UK government. Although some of the legal systems and requirements are unique to each of these nations, there are broad similarities in the legal structures across this geographical region. Therapists need to be familiar with the legal systems and requirements applicable to the area in which they live and work.

1.2 Introduction to the legal framework in England, Wales and Northern Ireland

1.2.1 Legal structure

The United Kingdom of Great Britain and Northern Ireland (UK) consists of four countries, with three distinct jurisdictions, each having its own court system and legal profession: England and Wales, Scotland and Northern Ireland. The UK is part of the European Union and is required to incorporate European legislation into UK law, and to recognise the jurisdiction of the European Court of Justice in matters of EU law.

The Queen is the Head of State, although in practice, the supreme authority of the Crown is carried by the government of the day. The Queen is advised by the Privy Council. The government comprises the Prime Minister (appointed by the Queen), the Ministers with departmental responsibilities, and those Ministers of State who form the Cabinet by the invitation of the Prime Minister. The legislature comprises the two Houses of Parliament – the House of Lords and the House of Commons.

In the UK, the constitutional law consists of the Acts of Parliament, known as 'statute law', subordinate legislation 'statutory instruments' made under the authority of the Acts of Parliament, and case law (the decisions of the courts), in which the courts interpret and apply the statute law. In case law, there is a hierarchy of court decisions, known as 'judicial precedent', in which the decisions of the House of Lords bind every court below it (including the Court of Appeal) and the decisions of the Court of Appeal bind all lower courts. See Figure 1.1 for an illustration of the hierarchy of the courts in England and Wales. There are also constitutional conventions which have binding force but do not have statutory authority.

1.2.2 The courts system

The courts are divided between criminal and civil. Criminal cases concern breaches of public morality of sufficient seriousness for the courts to be given powers to impose punishment on behalf of the state. Civil cases are largely about relationships between citizens and especially resolving any disputes that may arise.

Criminal trials

The magistrates' courts, which deal with minor offences, are the lowest criminal courts. More serious cases (trials on indictment) are committed for trial from the magistrates' court to be heard in the Crown Court (Queen's Bench Division). For discussion of disclosure of client notes and records, and giving evidence in criminal cases, please see Chapter 10 at 10.8, BACP Information Sheets G1 and G2 (Bond and Jenkins 2008; Bond et al. 2009), and detailed discussion in Bond and Sandhu (2005).

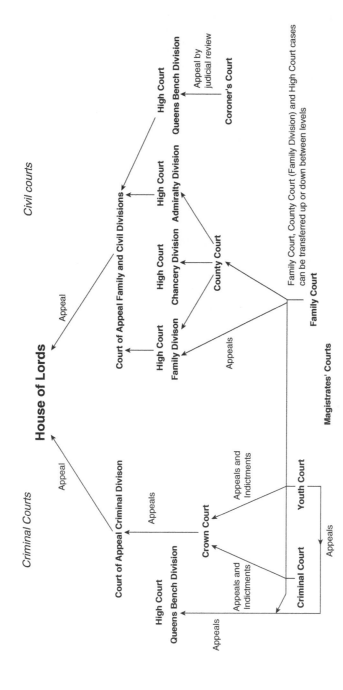

Figure 1.1 Hierarchy of the courts system in England and Wales and avenues of appeal

Criminal appeals

Subject to certain restrictions, a person convicted or sentenced in the magistrates' court may appeal to the Crown Court against conviction and/or sentence. Bail decisions may similarly be appealed. Appeals in criminal cases lie from the Crown Court to the Court of Appeal (Criminal Division). In some situations, appeal also lies from the magistrates' court or the Crown Court to the High Court, by way of 'case stated', that is requesting the magistrates' court or Crown Court to state the facts of a case and the questions of law or jurisdiction on which the opinion of the High Court is sought, see s. 111(1) of the Magistrates' Courts Act 1980, s. 28 of the Supreme Court Act 1981, and Part 52 of the Civil Procedure Rules 1998.

Civil cases

Therapists are probably most likely to be involved as witnesses in family or personal injury cases. Personal injury or negligence cases, like other civil matters (for minor claims), will at first instance be heard in the County Courts.

Parties who are dissatisfied with a judgment may appeal from the County Court to the High Court. More serious actions may be initiated in the High Court, which is divided into three divisions: Queen's Bench, Chancery and Family. Civil cases from the High Court may be appealed to the Court of Appeal (Civil Division). Details of Her Majesty's Courts Service and the work of the Tribunals can be found at www.hmcourts-service.gov.uk/.

The House of Lords is the supreme court of appeal. It has separate functions as a legislative body and as a court. Cases are heard by up to 13 senior judges known as the 'Law Lords'. Information about the judicial work and judgments of the House of Lords can be found at www.parliament.the-stationery-office.co.uk/pa/ld/ldjudinf.htm.

Children and family cases in the 'Family Court'

All children and family matters are dealt with in the 'Family Court', a new system created by the Children Act 1989. It has three tiers, the Family Proceedings Court (magistrates' level), the Family Division of the County Court, and the Family Division of the High Court. Cases can move up and down these levels as necessary. Child protection cases begin at the magistrates' level but may be transferred up and down as appropriate. The magistrates can hear some family cases. Appeals from the Family Proceedings Court, and most divorce, contact disputes, and most ancillary relief (finance and property) matters, will be heard in the County Court. Some appeals may go to the Family Division of the High Court, Court of Appeal and House of Lords.

Tribunals

In addition to the courts, there are specialised Tribunals, which hear appeals on decisions made by various public bodies and Government departments, in areas including employment, charities, immigration and social security, and the Criminal

Injuries Compensation Board, which adjudicates on compensation for injuries caused by criminals.

The courts system in Scotland

The courts system in Scotland is completely different from the system in England and Wales. Criminal cases are heard by the District Court, the Sheriff Court or the High Court of Justiciary, depending on the severity of the offence concerned. Serious cases, such as rape and murder, are dealt with at the High Court. The High Court of Justiciary also sits as an appeal court and determines criminal appeals. There is no right of appeal to the House of Lords in Scottish criminal cases, although there may be an appeal to the Privy Council in some circumstances.

Civil cases are heard at either the Sheriff Court or the Court of Session. Typically, the Sheriff Courts (situated throughout Scotland) deal with disputes of a lesser value. Cases of a high value are usually raised in the Court of Session in Edinburgh. The House of Lords is the supreme court of appeal in Scottish civil cases. Matters relating to child and family law can be dealt with in the Sheriff Court or in the Court of Session. Scotland also has a specialised Children's Hearings system with offices throughout the jurisdiction, dealing with certain matters relating to children. Employment Tribunals proceed in Scotland in the same way as in England.

1.2.3 Criminal and civil law

Law is often noticed in terms of crime, but in fact, the legal system comprises two sub-systems – civil and criminal law. The area covered by civil law is vast, regulating many aspects of our life and work. Glanville Williams refers to the distinction between a crime and a civil wrong as follows:

> ... the distinction does *not* reside in the nature of the wrongful act itself. This can be simply proved by pointing out that an act can be both a crime and a civil wrong ... but in the legal consequences that follow it. (sic)

He added, by way of explanation to law students:

> If the wrongful act is capable of being followed by what are called criminal proceedings, it is regarded as a crime. If it is capable of being followed by civil proceedings, that means that it is regarded as a civil wrong. If it is capable of being followed by both, it is both a crime and a civil wrong.

> (Glanville Williams 1963: 6)

An example of this might be a therapist who makes unwanted physical sexual advances to a client, which may constitute the criminal offence of assault (and also possibly a sexual offence), and may also give rise to a civil action for personal injury for the assault and any traumatic stress involved, not to mention grounds for complaint within the professional conduct procedure.

Criminal and civil proceedings are brought in different courts, with different procedure and terminology. Information can be found on the Lord Chancellor's website for citizens at www.direct.gov.uk/en/index.htm. Please see Chapter 10 on how to deal with legal claims in the various different courts.

Criminal law

Following a police investigation, the Crown Prosecution Service advises the police on evidence and law, and prepares the case for prosecution. The parties are referred to as the prosecutor and the defendant, or the accused.

Criminal cases are brought by the monarch against those accused, and so currently, they are referred to in court verbally as 'The Queen against … X'. This is written down as *R* (short for 'Regina' or 'Rex', meaning the Queen or King) v *X* (the defendant's surname or initial) with the date and the references for the various law reports in which they can be found, e.g. *R* v *H (Assault of Child: Reasonable Chastisement)* [2001] EWCA Crim 1024; [2001] 2 FLR 431.

In Scotland, cases are brought at the instance of the Crown in the High Court by Her Majesty's Advocate. They are reported as 'HMA v John Smith'. If the case is an appeal, the names are reversed so that the appeal decision is reported as 'John Smith v HMA'. Where the case is being brought in the Sheriff Court, it is brought by the area Procurator Fiscal as the representative of the Crown. These cases are sometimes referred to '*PF Edinburgh* v *John Smith*', and sometimes as (*Name of Fiscal*) v (*Name of Accused Person*). As in the High Court, the names are reversed for appeals.

Civil law

Civil cases are brought by an individual, company or organisation against another. The parties are referred to as applicant and respondent or plaintiff and defendant, and the cases cited as Re (in the matter of) X, with the date and the references for the various law reports in which they can be found, e.g. *Re W* [2008] EWCA Civ 538 [2008] All ER (D) 258 (May).

In Scotland, civil cases are simply reported using the names of the parties, e.g. John Smith v Jane Smith. The citation will depend on the series of law reports in which the case appears. For example, cases reported in the *Scots Law Times* will usually be cited as follows: *John Smith* v *Jane Smith* 1999 SLT 150. That citation means that the case report of *John Smith* v *Jane Smith* can be found in the 1999 volume of the *Scots Law Times*, with the report starting at page 150.

Lawyer

The term 'lawyer' is very wide and includes Queen's Counsel (QCs – senior barristers), barristers (members of the Bar), solicitors (solicitors of the Supreme Court) and legal executives (personnel qualified in law who may assist solicitors in the preparation of cases). In Scotland, members of the Bar are referred to as

advocates rather than barristers. There are also now 'paralegals' – other staff helping in the preparation of cases. The role of solicitors developed originally from
the early sixteenth century work of servants who helped barristers to prepare
cases. As a result, there developed a historical perception of a clear demarcation
between the roles of solicitor and barrister, coupled with a perception of the
social and intellectual superiority of the Bar, which still persisted well into the
1970s. Solicitors had limited rights of audience in certain courts. Barristers do not
personally interview witnesses, undertake case preparation or deal with client
money. They employ a clerk to deal with their administration and are given a
'brief' from their solicitor with instructions about their cases, on which they will
then advise, draft pleadings and provide advocacy in court. Currently, the distinction between the professional roles of barrister and solicitor is rapidly dimin-
ishing, with extended rights of advocacy for solicitors and the greater
employment of barristers in commercial and other fields. The judiciary at all levels are highly experienced lawyers, appointed for their expertise. They should be
independent of government and of politics. Most of the present senior judges
were formerly QCs, but the judiciary is now increasingly drawn from both
branches of the profession. For further information about lawyers, see the publications and websites of the Bar Council, the Law Society and the Judicial Studies
Board.

Evidence and the burden of proof

The rules of evidence are strict in every court, but they are different in criminal
and civil cases. The evidential rules are explained in this book wherever relevant
to the text. For discussion of therapists providing forensic reports, notes and evidence in court, see Chapter 10 and Bond and Sandhu (2005).

To secure a conviction in a criminal matter, the case for the prosecution has to
be proved beyond reasonable doubt.

The burden of proof in civil cases is on the balance of probabilities, i.e. 'that it is
more likely than not' that the events alleged actually occurred.

The courts require the 'best evidence', i.e. therapists' original contemporaneous
notes where possible (not just the neatly typed version made later on), and first-
hand witness evidence of events. Some courts therefore prohibit certain evidence
about character, 'hearsay' and opinion. If called to give evidence, ask the instructing solicitor beforehand about the rules of evidence that apply in that court.

The hearsay rule forbids a witness telling the court what someone else has said
in order to prove that it actually happened. For example, if the prosecution wants
to prove that Anne was assaulted by her partner John, either John has to admit his
guilt or the prosecution should produce evidence from Anne, or other witnesses
who actually saw the assault, to describe what happened. If Anne later tells her
therapist about the assault, that therapist's evidence in a criminal prosecution of
what Anne said during counselling might be relevent but will not by itself prove
that the event described really happened.

There is an important exception to the hearsay rule where child law cases are concerned. In these cases, the court wants to have all the evidence that is available, and so hearsay evidence is allowed. Section 96(3) of the Children Act 1989 and the Children (Admissibility of Hearsay Evidence) Order 1993 ST 1993/621 provide that in civil proceedings before the High Court or a county court, family proceedings, and civil proceedings in a magistrates' court under the Child Support Act 1991, evidence given in connection with the upbringing, maintenance or welfare of a child shall be admissible notwithstanding any rule of law relating to hearsay. The implication of this is that where children (or family members) are in therapy, especially in situations where that child or family may be involved in court proceedings, it is important that careful and accurate notes of sessions should be made, since the therapist could potentially be asked in court to repeat what has been said if it is relevant to a child's welfare, maintenance or upbringing. Examples might include a therapist working with:

- a client who, in the course of therapy, admits being an active paedophile and talks about their activities, which harm children or place children at risk of harm
- a child who has experienced abuse and is subject to child protection proceedings
- a parent involved in an intractable contact dispute
- a child who has a medical or psychiatric condition requiring urgent treatment, but which is refused by the child or those with parental responsibility.

These therapists could potentially be asked to give evidence or produce notes in criminal prosecutions, child protection or any other proceedings involving the upbringing, maintenance or welfare of a child. Such disclosures may be ordered by a court. Disclosures made even without client consent, to prevent a real risk of imminent and serious harm, could potentially be justifiable in the public interest (see Chapter 10 and Bond and Mitchels 2008).

The hearsay rule applies in criminal cases, so in a prosecution, the therapist would not be asked to give hearsay evidence to prove the case, although their evidence may be relevant to the case in some other way. For detailed discussion of evidence, reports and going to court, see *Therapists in Court* (Bond and Sandhu 2005).

1.3 Working within the law

Therapists should work professionally in compliance with the law. This might sound straightforward in theory but this can sometimes be much more difficult to accomplish in practice, since the law is constantly evolving and in some areas the law is uncertain or even seemingly contradictory. For example, in medical practice, doctors are allowed to use their discretion in providing treatment but (although the courts remain reluctant to interfere in medical matters) their conduct remains open to legal challenge.

With the exception of a situation where the law requires disclosure, e.g. terrorism, therapists may use their discretion in making decisions about breaching confidentiality, for example in situations of child protection, self-harm or certain suspected less serious criminal activity. Such decisions are complex and may be open to questioning and require justification if legally challenged after the event. (See Bond and Mitchels (2008), in which we explore options and potential dilemmas in decision-making, considering the alternatives and the consequences of each, so that therapists can make their own informed decisions.) For detailed information on responding to requests for disclosure and giving evidence in court, please see *Therapists in Court* (Bond and Sandhu 2005). In Chapter 10 of this book, to defuse some of the fear of the unknown, we share insights from our experience of going to court, including hints on court etiquette and how to address the magistrates or judge.

2 Public Interest and Professional Standards

How do I balance my therapeutic relationship with the client with my professional responsibilities?

I don't know what my professional duties are exactly – I can't find a clear list of them anywhere...

Can the government, my professional organisation or my supervisor actually stop me from practising as a counsellor/psychotherapist?

How does membership of a professional organisation help me? Is membership of benefit to my clients?

I don't know how I feel about regulation – what would it really mean to me in practice?

The present political climate is one of increasing government control of standards of practice in the provision of publicly funded services, and also services to vulnerable members of the public. The trend towards the protection of some citizens has tended to blur the traditional distinctions between law controlling public bodies and actions by the populace (public law) and private legal transactions between people and organisations (private law). Nonetheless there are still areas of law where the guiding principle remains 'let the buyer beware'. For example, in contract law (see Chapter 4) the Latin phrase *caveat emptor*, meaning 'buyer beware', warns the buyer to be careful about understanding and negotiating the detailed terms of contracts, especially those for commercial services. In contrast, services provided by public bodies are usually directly regulated by government. The provision of health services by the NHS, for example, is regulated to ensure adherence to certain standards of health care and to provide a degree of public liability. Where services are provided to the public by private bodies, for example, day care for children or adoption services, the government may set guidelines and regulate standards, which may include strict conditions in contracts for services.

Typically, counselling and psychotherapy services that are funded by public bodies such as the NHS or local authorities are provided by commercial or not-for-profit organisations which are bound by their 'service provider' contracts to conform to the procedures and standards that legally apply to their sponsoring body. The areas covered by regulation are rapidly widening and there is a strong possibility that counselling and psychotherapy will become government-regulated professions in the future – current estimates suggest some time around 2012.

Therapists wishing to achieve and maintain best practice standards have already formed their own self-regulating organisations. Some are linked with specific therapeutic orientations and others include diverse modalities, e.g. BACP, which currently has over 33,000 members from a wide variety of therapeutic approaches. BACP, as part of its service to members, provides guidance in the form of books, Information Sheets journals, research information, training, a web-site and opportunities for practitioners to meet together, share experiences and information, and network at conferences and other events.

In addition, BACP has developed ethical standards for membership, accreditation and registration of practitioners. BACP members agree to work within the *Ethical Framework* (BACP 2010) and accept the authority of BACP in the implementation of its disciplinary procedures. Other professional organisations have similar systems and conditions of membership, which serve to protect the public by maintaining professional standards. In some cases the government imposes statutory control and regulation. For example, therapists working in the health professions may be subject to statute, and the regulations and procedures set by the British Medical Association and the General Medical Council (see for example, GMC 2004).

Since therapists are generally concerned for the protection of clients in addition to meeting their own needs, members of BACP (and other professional organisations) accept that, should they fall below the required standards, they may be subject to the relevant disciplinary procedures and that they may be asked to demonstrate that they have improved their practice by undergoing further training. In certain more serious cases, their membership may be suspended or terminated. In cases where employment depends upon membership, temporary suspension or permanent loss of membership status may result in the loss of work. For details of the membership, accreditation and registration requirements, the disciplinary code, and the *Ethical Framework*, see the BACP website at www.bacp.org.uk.

Government regulation aims to protect the public who use certain services by providing formal benchmarks for professional standards and by providing a degree of quality control of practitioners providing those services. In addition, regulation seeks to ensure that the quality of the services provided is improved by postgraduate training, development of specialist knowledge, or continuing professional and personal development.

At the moment, counselling and psychotherapy are not government-regulated professions, although they are still subject to various forms of overt (and also less immediately obvious) government control, e.g. the law against terrorism and the direct effects of the treatment recommendations of NICE within the health service, and indirect influences on other types of service. Those therapists working within the health care services must comply with wider regulation and standards, e.g. the provision of access to health records under the Data Protection Act 1998, the Freedom of Information Act 2000, and internal government agency procedures for the protection of vulnerable adults and children (see Chapters 3, 4 and 9; see also Bond and Mitchels 2008).

Therapists, although mainly unregulated, nevertheless have duties and responsibilities to their clients arising in public and private law. This chapter maps out the legal duties and responsibilities of therapists to their clients in the context of a variety of therapeutic settings and relationships, cross-referencing them to the places in this book where they are explored in greater detail.

In all therapeutic situations, the following duties exist.

- Duty to provide appropriate professional standards of therapeutic care (see Chapter 3)
- Confidentiality, subject to specific contractual agreements and to the law (see Chapters 3, 4, 5 and 9; Bond and Mitchels 2008; and BACP Information Sheets G1 *Access to Records* (Bond and Jenkins 2008) and G2 *Breaches in Confidentiality* (Bond et al. 2009)).

In specific therapeutic situations, the following additional duties exist.

2.1 Private practitioners

In relation to the work undertaken, private practitioners need to pay attention to:

- training, qualifications and continuing professional development
- insurance
- premises
- contracting with clients
- contracts of employment when working within agencies
- partnership agreements when working with other therapists to provide a service
- information sharing and data protection issues
- facilities and resources to support the work
- national and local law.

2.2 Non-government agencies and organisations (NGOs)

In relation to the work undertaken, non-government agencies and organisations need to pay attention to:

- training, qualifications and continuing professional development
- employee/volunteer contracts
- development of NGO agency policies and procedures
- government guidance
- data protection and information sharing
- insurance
- premises
- contracting with clients
- facilities and resources to support the work
- national and local law.

2.3 Government agencies and organisations

In addition to many of the issues listed in 2.2 above, government agencies and organisations must comply with:

- statutory law that enables the state to provide specific services such as health care, education, social services, prisons etc.
- internal government guidance, regulations, policies and procedures
- Freedom of Information Act 2000
- Data Protection Act 1998, Data Protection (Subjects Access Modification) (Health) Order 2000, and the Data Protection (Processing of Sensitive Personal Data) Order 2000 (see Chapters 3, 4 and 9; Bond and Mitchels 2008).

2.4 Supervision

The respective duties of the supervisor and supervisee will depend in part on their professional modality, their contract of supervision and the organisational setting within which they work (i.e. whether, for example, they work in an organisation in which they have a managerial relationship as well as a supervisory one) (see BACP 2004, 2009; Feltham, 1999; Hackney and Goodyear 1984; Hawkins and Shoet 1996; Jacobs 1996; Mearns 2004a, b; Page and Wosket 1998).

> As a Supervisor, you have to encompass many functions in your role. In part you are a counsellor giving support; also you are an educator helping the supervisee learn and develop, and in many situations you are also a manager with responsibilities both for what the supervisee is doing with and to the client and also to the organisation within which you both work.
>
> (Hawkins and Shoet 1996: 37)

There are potential problems in combining the roles of supervision and management, which are of concern to BACP:

> Choosing a line manager as supervisor can lead to difficulties since a conflict of interests may arise between the needs of the unit or institution (the priority of the line manager) and the needs of the counsellor [or the client]. If line management supervision is mandatory, then there must be access to other consultative support.
>
> (BACP 2004)

Potential conflicts of interest may arise, for example, within voluntary or charitable organisations providing counselling services, where the counsellors are line-managed by the Director or other officer of the organisation, who may also provide group or individual supervision. There may be in-house supervisors who are funded by the organisation and contractually bound to it, and also (to varying degrees) subject to the control of the organisational management. It is worth considering the possible issues of dual roles (see BACP Information Sheet G3, *Dual Roles* (Jacobs 2007)).

In supervision, the supervisee's needs and interests are an essential focus of the work but, as Page and Wosket (1998) point out, the welfare of the supervisee's client is of primary importance, especially where the client is at risk. This is different from counselling, in which the work centres on the client and the client/counsellor relationship.

In supervision, practitioners need to create a balance between the legal and professional boundaries of supervision with the supervisee's obligations under their client contracts and the other overarching legal duties and responsibilities which apply to both the supervisor and supervisee (e.g. in criminal law, negligence, child protection, etc.). Both need to be aware of overarching issues such as legal limitations, public interest, confidentiality and how to share information between professionals appropriately (see Bond 1990; Bond and Mitchels 2008: Chapters 5 and 9).

The supervisor has a contractual duty and responsibility to the supervisee. The supervisor has no direct contractual relationship with the supervisee's client(s), but holds the responsibility to oversee the supervisee's practice for the benefit of the supervisee's clients. While a supervisor should not be overly prescriptive, but facilitative, there are times when authoritative action or advice about best practice, including ethics or law, is necessary. For example, when a client is at risk and an inexperienced supervisee needs guidance or direction about when or how to make an appropriate disclosure or a referral, or when working with trainees or therapists who are inexperienced in specific issues for their current casework, the following advice is legally sound:

> ...a supervisor needs to be prepared to carry a more readily identifiable authority which includes monitoring the practice of the supervisee. This does involve assessment, judgment, and on occasion being prescriptive about what the other person should or should not do.
>
> (Page and Wosket 1998: 22)

In the context of supervision, the supervisor has responsibility for monitoring and evaluating the quality of the counselling practice of the supervisee, e.g. to watch for burn-out in highly stressful areas of work, or when working with difficult or demanding clients, or where work levels are high (see Bauer, Hafner et al. 2003). This responsibility is increased in a situation where supervision includes an element of management. Supervisees also have their own duty, within the supervisory relationship, to constantly monitor and evaluate their own practice (Proctor 1986).

The supervisor and the supervisee have a contractual relationship with each other in which the supervisor has (among other responsibilities) a duty of care to the supervisee. The counsellor's own separate contractual relationship with their client also includes a duty of care (see Chapter 3 generally and at 3.10, for the supervisor's potential liability in tort).

The supervisor does not have a direct contractual relationship with the supervisee's client, but nevertheless has an ethical responsibility to attend to that client's welfare in supervision. This means in law that a supervisor may be sued for breach of contract by a supervisee, but not by the supervisee's client.

However, in the law of tort (see Chapter 3 at 3.10), if the chain of causation could be proved, the supervisor could, in theory, potentially be accountable to the supervisee and their clients in the context of their role in relation to a client who has been brought to the supervision and in respect of whom the supervisor had provided therapeutically incorrect or unhelpful advice or guidance which was then acted upon by the supervisee to the detriment of the client. A claim of this sort against a supervisor would be difficult to establish in law, and we are not aware of any such action brought in England and Wales (see Chapter 3 at 3.10).

We are, however, aware of a supervisor being brought into the complaints procedure by a counsellor's professional organisation to discuss ethical responsibilities. In any legal case based on the alleged professional negligence of a supervisor, appropriate legal advice should be sought on the specific circumstances of that case. For further discussion, see Chapters 3 (Negligence), 4 (Contract), 6 (Insurance), and 9 (Employment).

In employment or in training situations, the supervisor may be expected or specifically contractually bound to report any concern arising where the supervisee is unfit to work, or where the standard of the supervisee's work falls below that expected of a competent professional. Equally, a supervisor is held legally responsible to their supervisees and to any organisations concerned for the accuracy and professional competency of any reports made for accreditation, registration, fellowship or disciplinary purposes.

For supervisees in training, see 2.5 below.

2.5 Training

Where a supervisee is in training, the supervision contract should also address, where relevant, the boundaries of supervision in relation to that training.

A recognised supervisor for a training organisation may be required to submit regular reports of the supervisee's progress, which may be shared with the supervisee and discussed in advance of submission. The supervisee may expect to read these reports and to be able to add their own comments. As noted in 2.4. above, the supervisor may also have accepted a contractual duty to share with the organisation any serious concerns about the trainee's work or health (mental or physical) which may interfere with the supervisee's ability to function effectively in counselling.

It is possible in law that a trainee who has suffered quantifiable damage of some sort can take legal action against their training organisation or their trainer, alleging, for example, that the trainer has breached their duty of care by paying inadequate attention to the trainee's academic or psychological needs, thereby causing damage or loss to the trainee. A training organisation in a contractual relationship with its trainees will have a duty of professional care which may include both the organisation and its trainers. The duty of care to trainees must be balanced by the trainers' other contractual and ethical responsibilities for assessment and reporting. See Chapters 3 (Tort) and 4 (Contract) for further discussion.

Where supervisees need to work with video- or audio-recordings of client sessions in supervision or in training, issues arise concerning the client's confidentiality when tapes are shared (see Bond and Mitchels 2008: chapter 5). Typical questions we are asked include the following.

Should I tell the client why the recording is being made?
Consider why the recording is being made. Who asked for it and who will benefit from it? For example, is it to assist the counsellor in training, supervision or educational purposes, or just as an aide memoire? Is it intended as an aid to therapy for both client and therapist?

What therapeutic issues are there about the making of recordings? For example, does the client have an issue with former abuse that involved some sort of recording or photography? Is the client fearful of recordings and potential disclosures?

Remember that all client notes and records may be required in court proceedings, including any recordings made. If a therapist proposes to record sessions, there is an ethical and legal duty of care to the client, which includes making the client fully aware of the purpose, and what may happen to the recording. In all cases, the client should first give explicit consent to the recording being made, with full knowledge of its potential uses. This is also a statutory requirement where the Freedom of Information Act 2000 or the Data Protection Act 1998 applies (see Bond and Mitchels 2008, Chapters 3 and 6).

Who owns the recordings?
Legally, ownership of the recording vests in the person who owns the physical medium on which the recording exists (e.g. the tape, CD, DVD, etc.), unless otherwise specifically agreed. However, the *content* of the recording is regulated according to the contractual agreement between the parties who made the recording, i.e. client and therapist, on two counsellors in training, etc.

Where should recordings be kept?
Clients and counsellors may agree between themselves about labelling, storage, security and confidentiality, unless they are both bound by agency policies.

Can the client refuse consent to make a recording?
The client has a contractual right to refuse recording, provided that they have mental capacity (see Chapter 4; and Bond and Mitchels 2008: chapter 11).

Does the client have the legal right to listen to their own recordings? Who else has the right to listen to them?
Recordings are part of the client record and therefore subject to disclosure to the client and to others where required by the law (see Bond and Mitchels 2008: Chapters 3, 4 and 9). They are also subject to the terms of the therapeutic contract.

Can clients request to keep their recordings or to destroy their recordings if they so wish?
This depends on the legal ownership of the recordings and any statutory or contractual duty to retain records for any specific length of time. If they are owned by the client, then the client may do with them as they wish (unless otherwise agreed with the therapist). If there is an agency or statutory duty that applies to the recording, for example if it forms part of a mental health record, then those provisions govern what happens to the record.

Therapists and clients should discuss and agree in their therapeutic contract what they will do with any recordings that they make. For discussion of contracts, see Chapter 4 of this book, and for mental health records, also see Bond and Mitchels (2008: Chapters 7, 9 and 10). Where explicit consent is required for the making, storage and use of recordings, this should form part of the client or the supervision contract and, for the avoidance of doubt, the client's explicit consent should be obtained where appropriate and necessary.

2.6 Compliance with professional standards and 'whistle-blowing' on bad practice

This is one of the areas where morality, ethics and law meet, and sometimes the boundaries between them seem unclear. No professional is likely to feel entirely happy about reporting the bad practice or professional misconduct of another person, especially a colleague with whom they work. However, in some situations, 'whistle-blowing' may be necessary to maintain good professional practice, and it may be permitted or even required within agency policy (contractually agreed by all the agency's employees) or required by law (e.g. reporting terrorist activities under the Terrorism Act 2000 or by an order of a court).

There are other situations where whistle-blowing is not specifically required by law or agency policy, but is left to the therapist's discretion. These may include situations where colleagues discover criminal acts (e.g. a therapist sexually assaulting clients or mistreating vulnerable adults), or they may witness bad practice leading to the risk of potential harm to a child or vulnerable adult, where therapists might feel that whistle-blowing is morally justified. The issue then for the therapist is whether whistle-blowing is *legally* defensible, for example, in the public interest (i.e. that the protection of the general public may justifiably outweigh personal or private rights, such as confidentiality).

Bear in mind that the law prohibits attacks on the reputation of another and court cases can be brought for slander (untrue verbal allegations damaging the reputation of another) and libel (similar untrue and damaging allegations made in writing), but a defence to both of these would be that the allegations made were true and made in the public interest.

In the case of bad professional practice, where a colleague has been clearly warned about their conduct and has failed to make changes, or where the colleague conceals their conduct from management or their professional organisation, practitioners may feel that whistle-blowing may be the only way left to stop the bad practice continuing.

2.7 Protection of children and vulnerable adults

The government has issued statutes, subsidiary legislation and guidance to protect the interests of children and vulnerable adults. In many areas of work, for example, the NHS, schools and residential homes, staff have to comply with vetting procedures, details of which are set out in Chapter 5 at 5.11.

2.7.1 Risk to children

Child protection legislation now uses the term 'Risk to children'. Home Office Circular 16/2005 (*Guidance on offences against children*) explains how those people who present a risk, or potential risk, of harm to children should be identified. The new list of offences should be used as a 'trigger' to a further assessment to determine if an offender should be regarded as presenting a continued risk of harm to children. An offender who has harmed a child might not necessarily continue to present a risk towards that child or other children.

Once an individual has been sentenced and identified as presenting a risk to children, agencies have a responsibility to work collaboratively to monitor and manage the risk of harm to others. In cases where the offender has been sentenced to a period of custody, prison establishments undertake a similar responsibility and, in addition, notify other agencies prior to any period of release.

Multi Agency Public Protection Arrangements (MAPPA) provided a national framework in England and Wales for the assessment and management of risk posed by serious and violent offenders, including individuals who are considered to pose a risk, or potential risk, of harm to children. The arrangements impose statutory requirements on the police and probation services (the 'Responsible Authorities') to make these arrangements under ss. 67–68 of the Criminal Justice and Court Services Act 2000 and ss. 325–327 of the Criminal Justice Act 2003. The development of national databases significantly enhances the capability to track offenders who move between communities and across organisational boundaries. The full MAPPA guidance is available at: www.probation.homeoffice.gov.uk/output/page30.asp.

This system will be superseded by the new Vetting and Barring Scheme under the Safeguarding Vulnerable Groups Act 2006 – see Chapter 5.11 at 5.11 for details. That section also explains other government lists and Criminal Records Bureau (CRB) and Criminal Records Bureau Scotland (CRBS) checks.

2.7.2 The Sex Offenders Register and statutory protective orders

Notification under Part 2 of the Sexual Offences Act 2003 (known as the Sex Offenders Register) is an automatic requirement on offenders who receive a conviction or caution for certain sexual offences. The notification requirements are intended to ensure that the police are informed of the whereabouts of offenders in the community. Offenders must notify the police of certain personal details within three days of their conviction or caution for a relevant sexual offence (or, if they are in prison on this date, within three days of their release). All offenders must reconfirm their details at least once every 12 months, and notify the police seven days in advance of any travel overseas for a period of three days or more. The period of time for which an offender must comply with these requirements depends on whether they received a conviction or caution for their offence and, where appropriate, the sentence they received. Failure to comply with these requirements is a criminal offence, with a maximum penalty of five years' imprisonment. British citizens or residents, as well as foreign nationals, can be placed on the Sex Offenders Register in the UK if they receive convictions or cautions for sexual offences overseas.

Sexual Offences Prevention Orders may be made when a court deals with an offender convicted for violent and other offences and assessed as posing a risk of serious sexual harm. They may include prohibitions, e.g. from loitering near schools or playgrounds.

Introduced by the Sexual Offences Act 2003, *Risk of Sexual Harm Orders* are used to protect children from the risks posed by individuals who do not necessarily have a previous conviction for a sexual or violent offence but who have, on at least two occasions, engaged in sexually explicit conduct or communication with a child or children, and who pose a risk of further such harm. They may, for example, prohibit the person from using certain internet chat rooms.

2.7.3 Compliance with statutory protective procedures

Therapists who are on any of these lists, or who are subject to any of these protective orders, must comply with the legislation.

Part 1 of *Working Together to Safeguard Children* (DfES 2006c) is statutory guidance issued under s. 7 of the Local Authority Social Services Act 1970 and must be complied with by local authorities carrying out their social services functions. Part 2 is non-statutory practice guidance.

In cases where *Working Together to Safeguard Children* is not statutory guidance for a particular organisation, it still represents a standard of good practice. For example, managers and staff in educational institutions and those in organisations and agencies with a duty to safeguard and promote the welfare of children under s. 11 of the Children Act 2004 (found at: www.everychildmatters.gov.uk/socialcare/safeguarding/) are encouraged to read this document and follow it in conjunction with the guidance on that duty.

Therefore, therapists who train or supervise others, or who work with colleagues or clients to whom these lists or protective orders may apply, should pay careful attention to the Guidance set out in Chapter 12 of the *Working Together to Safeguard Children* (DfES 2006c), and to the provisions of the Safeguarding Vulnerable Groups Act 2006 (see Mitchels, B. (2009) 'Safeguarding vulnerable groups', *Therapy Today* 20(9): 26–30).

3 Liability in Tort: Negligence

I have read about therapists being sued for negligence in the USA. Is the law with regard to negligence different here in the UK?

What does the duty of care actually mean, and to whom do I owe it?

In what sort of situations could the law say that I have been negligent?

If I have acted carelessly or, maybe even recklessly, but not really meaning to cause any harm, would I still be liable in law?

Do supervisors have a duty of care to their supervisee's clients as well as to their supervisees?

Can a third party sue the therapist for negligence – for instance a member of the client's family?

If I think I have done something wrong, would an apology put me at risk?

How can I protect myself from claims for negligence?

3.1 What is the law of tort?

The law of tort in England and Wales is the general law of civil liability (in Scotland, it is called 'delict'). The word 'tort' (colloquially meaning injustice) was probably imported into our law from old French, having evolved from the Medieval Latin *tortum* derived from *torquēre* (to twist) and *tortus* (meaning twisted, crooked, dubious). The Scottish term delict, like much of the Scottish legal system, has its origins in Roman law. Over the years, the law of tort came to cover many injustices, and developed what Oliphant (2007: 1) delightfully describes as 'a ragbag character', including liability for accidental injury, interference with a person's liberty, reputation or dominion over his body, goods, land or economic interests. The principal remedies available for breach of the law of tort are injunctions (orders not to do something) and damages (financial awards by the court). Tort law does not include employment, contract or commercial law, which are separate – they govern work, business and service agreements, including therapeutic contracts (see Chapter 4). The 'ragbag' of the law of tort includes the important concepts of negligence and recklessness, and this chapter explores how these might apply to the day-to-day practice of counselling and psychotherapy.

3.2 Do I have to intend to cause harm to be liable in tort? What if I did not mean to cause harm, or if I did not foresee what happened?

Tort is a complicated area of law, and legal liability does not always depend on malicious intent. A person might also be liable in tort without deliberately intending to cause any harm, or through a reckless or inadvertent act or omission, which, although unintentional, may nevertheless constitute a lack of the required standard of professional care.

Liability in tort arises when:

- there is interference with a claimant's protected interests
- caused by the defendant or by someone for whose acts the defendant is responsible
- conduct occurs that justifies financial compensation or an injunction.

'Protected interests' in tort law include the person, personal property, land and financial well-being, and rights of an intangible nature such as autonomy, liberty, reputation and privacy. 'Caused' can mean intentionally, or unintentionally, either negligently or recklessly. 'Conduct' includes both acts and omissions.

Examples of actions that may give rise to complaints and/or claims in tort are explored in 3.5 below.

3.3 What is a duty of care?

Legal liability will in some circumstances depend upon the legal concept of a 'duty of care'.

The House of Lords considered the issue in the case of *Phelps* v *Hillingdon London Borough Council* [2000] 3 WLR 776. This was part of a group of four appeals, all heard together, to decide whether a duty of care was owed by educational psychologists to a child (and/or to the child's parents) concerning their failure to diagnose dyslexia. The damage claimed arose from the impact of this failure upon the children concerned.

Lord Slynn of Hadley commented:

> …it is long and well-established, now elementary, that persons exercising a particular skill or profession may owe a duty of care in the performance to people who it can be foreseen will be injured if due skill and care are not exercised, and if injury or damage can be shown to have been caused by the lack of care. Such duty does not depend on the existence of any contractual relationship between the person causing and the person suffering the damage. A doctor, an accountant and an engineer are plainly such a person. So in my view is an educational psychologist or psychiatrist and a teacher including a teacher in a specialised area, such as a teacher concerned with children having special educational needs.

By analogy with the educational psychologist in that case, a counsellor, psychotherapist, coach, etc. will all owe a duty of care to their clients and supervisees to carry out the task of therapy with due skill and professional competence.

3.4 When do I owe a duty of care and to whom do I owe it?

The House of Lords, in *Phelps* v *Hillingdon London Borough Council*, made it clear that not only is a duty of care owed to those in a contractual relationship, but, in some circumstances, it will also be owed to third parties. In addition to Lord Slynn's definition of the duty of care (cited in 3.3 above), their Lordships held that:

(1) … where an educational psychologist was specifically asked to advise as to the assessment of and future provision for a child and it was clear that the child's parents and teachers would follow that advice, a duty of care prima facie arose; that the local educa- tion authority was prima facie vicariously liable for a breach of that duty … and that the relationship between the plaintiff and the educational psychologist employed by the defendant authority in the first case and the task she had been doing had created the necessary nexus to place the psychologist under a duty of care to the plaintiff and the judge had been entitled to hold her in breach of that duty and that the authority was vic- ariously liable for that breach.

(2) That a failure to mitigate the adverse consequences of a congenital defect such as dyslexia was capable of constituting 'personal injuries to a person' within section 33(2) of the Supreme Court Act 1981.

Considering the responsibility of the educational psychologist, Lord Slynn of Hadley commented:

It must still be shown that the educational psychologist is acting in relation to a particular child in a situation where the law recognises a duty of care. A casual remark, an isolated act may occur in a situation where there is no sufficient nexus between the two persons for a duty of care to exist. But where an educational psychologist is specifically called in to advise in relation to the assessment and future provision for a specific child, and it is clear that the parents acting for the child and the teachers will follow that advice, prima facie a duty of care arises. It is sometimes said that there has to be an assumption of responsibility by the person concerned …

 There can be no doubt that if foreseeability and causation are established, psychological injury may constitute damage for the purpose of the common law. But so in my view can a failure to diagnose a congenital condition and to take appropriate action as a result of which failure a child's level of achievement is reduced, which leads to loss of employment and wages.

For discussion of a duty of care which may be owed to third parties, see 3.9 and for the special case of responsibility and liability in the context of supervision, see 3.10 below.

3.5 What sort of harm might be the subject of a claim in tort in the context of therapy?

Tortious actions defined in English civil law include:

* negligence
* battery (assault)

- trespass (to goods or persons)
- conversion (one aspect of wrongful interference with goods).

The law in Scotland differs significantly in areas such as assault, trespass and wrongful interference with goods. However, it is fair to say that Scottish law recognises the same types of harm on which a claim may be based in delict as those which could give rise to a claim in tort in England and Wales.

Although the NHS deals with a substantial number of claims against medical practitioners, there have been (so far!) very few legal cases against therapists in the UK. We can, however, gain some insights from leading legal cases against therapists in the USA, and from the medical cases from England and Wales that might be comparable in some ways to the work of therapy. Most of the UK cases come from healthcare, i.e. medical and psychiatric treatment, and many of these can be relevant to therapeutic practice.

Often, actions which are potentially negligent are also breaches of the therapeutic contract. See Chapter 4 at 4.4, for further discussion of this.

We are grateful to the insurers, Towergate Professional, for their assistance in telling us about common categories of actions or omissions by therapists which are the subject of complaint or legal action. We have set out some of these in Table 3.1. The table shows that these actions are contrary to the *Ethical Framework* (BACP 2010). Many are also in breach of the therapeutic contract, and some have resulted in successful claims against therapists in court. Many of these misdemeanours are boundary violations in various forms. They include: sexual contact, offers of friendship, inappropriate touch, bullying or disrespect, emotional or financial exploitation, inappropriate disclosures, inappropriate encounters with others, giving and receiving of gifts and professional incompetence.

Further examples of potential torts below are taken from decided medical negligence cases, describing circumstances which, by analogy, might also be encountered in the context of therapeutic practice:

- Therapeutic treatment given without appropriate consent (see the case of *R (B)* v *(1) Dr SS (2) Dr G (3) Secretary of State for the Health Department [Admin. Ct.]* [2005] 1 MHLR 347).
- Treating a client for the wrong thing or treating a person in the wrong way for them, causing damage in the process (see the case of *R (B)* v *Ashworth Hospital Authority* [HL] [2005] 1 MHLR 47, where the issue was whether a patient detained under the classification of mental illness should have been treated on a ward for those suffering from personality disorder).
- Breach of a client's confidence, whether deliberately or inadvertently (see the case of *W* v *Egdell* [1989] 1 All ER 1089; [1990] Ch 359; [1990] 1All ER 835; [1990] 2 WLR 471 where the issue was whether breach of confidence was defensible in the public interest). Breach of confidence may constitute a breach of contract as well as a potential ground for a claim in tort.
- Harassment, whether among colleagues at work or towards clients (see *Khorasandjian* v *Bush* [1993] 3 WLR 476 (Court of Appeal)).

Table 3.1   Therapist acts, ommissions and potential consequences

Actions by therapist towards client	BACP *Ethical Framework* principles	Potential ground for complaint	Potential breach of contract	Has resulted in court finding of negligence or malpractice
Professional incompetence	Fidelity, autonomy, justice, self-respect, beneficence, non-maleficence	Yes	Yes	Yes
Inappropriate sexual contact	Fidelity, autonomy, beneficence, non-maleficence, self-respect	Yes	Yes	Yes
Emotional or financial exploitation	Fidelity, autonomy, beneficence, non-maleficence, self-respect	Yes	Yes	Yes
Bullying or disrespect	Fidelity, autonomy, beneficence, non-maleficence	Yes	Yes	Yes
Offers of friendship	Fidelity, autonomy, beneficence, non-maleficence, self-respect	Yes	Yes	
Inappropriate touch	Fidelity, autonomy, beneficence, non-maleficence, self-respect	Yes	Yes	
Inappropriate encounters with others at place of therapy	Autonomy, fidelity, non-maleficence	Yes	Yes	
Inappropriate self-disclosures by therapist	Autonomy, fidelity, non-maleficence, self-respect	Yes		
Giving and receiving gifts	Autonomy, fidelity, self-respect	Yes		

Peter Jenkins (2007: 76) has unearthed some interesting cases (mainly related to sexual and/or breach of confidentiality issues) brought against therapists in the USA (from Feldman and Ward 1979; Kermani 1989; Otto and Schmidt 1991). These include:

- having a relationship with the client's wife (*Mazza* v *Huffaker* [1983] 300 SE2d 833 (NC))
- having an affair with a client – woman part of a couple in marital counselling (*Nicholsen* v *Han* [1968] 12 Mich. App. 35, 162 NW 2d 313)
- having an affair with a client as part of therapy as an alleged attempt to overcome the client's lesbianism (*Roy* v *Hartogs* [1975]: 366 NYS 297, 300–301)
- therapists (Roe and Roe) writing a book about their conjoint therapeutic work with their former clients who were the claimant and her late husband (*Doe* v *Roe and Roe* [1977]; 400 NY p2d 668).

3.6 Negligence

3.6.1 What constitutes negligence?

In 3.3, the 'duty of care' was considered. The legal concept of negligence is based on the breach of appropriate professional standards and/or of a duty of care, causing damage. In law, in order to prove a case of negligence, lawyers refer to the 'nexus of causation' – meaning the degree of connection between the negligence alleged and proof that the damage suffered by the claimant was actually caused by it. In order to establish a case against a therapist, the plaintiff would have to prove:

- that a duty of care exists
- a breach of that duty of care (conduct falling below the standards that the law demands)
- in the case of advice, that the defendant could have foreseen that any advice given would be relied upon (foreseeability)
- that, as a result of the action/omission complained of, the plaintiff suffered damage
- that the actions/omissions complained of were the cause of the damage.

The court would need proof of damage that could be redressed somehow by financial compensation or an injunction. Damage could include psychiatric illness, but perhaps not necessarily hurt feelings, i.e. 'mere grief, distress and upset' (see *McLoughlin* v *O'Brian* [1983] 1 AC 410 at 431).

Jenkins (2007: 79–80) discusses the interesting UK case of *Werner* v *Landau* [1961] Times Law Reports 8 March 1961, in which the claimant had alleged that Dr Werner, a psychiatrist, had treated her between March and August 1949, and then treated her again from March 1950 to January 1951. In all he had provided some 24 sessions of psychotherapy. The problem was that between the two sets of sessions, Dr Werner and she had exchanged letters, he had visited her flat, and they had even discussed going away for a weekend together. Ms Landau later alleged that there had been sexual misconduct by Dr Werner, but the court dismissed this as an 'erotic fantasy'. In April 1951, Ms Landau attempted suicide. Much later, she sued

Dr Werner for damages, accusing him of clinical negligence. His defence was that their social contact was necessary for her welfare, and/or that the damage Ms Landau suffered was due to either a pre-existing condition or external intervening factors. The Court of Appeal (despite the judges' rejection of the sexual misconduct allegations) was greatly assisted by documentary evidence which included the parties' letters. It rejected both Dr Werner's defence and his appeal, affirming that the psychological and financial damage suffered by Ms Landau was caused by his negligence.

Many instances of alleged negligence are the subject of complaints to professional bodies, and some are the subject of legal claims. Out of those legal claims that may be brought before the courts, it seems that many, if not most of them, are settled out of court. Out of those few court cases that proceed to a full hearing and judgment, only a few will be included in the main UK law reports. All this means that we have very few reported court cases from the UK on negligence in the context of therapy to provide guidance, but by looking at the experience of insurers, we can at least gain some insight into the types of actions or omissions which might give rise to complaints or to legal claims.

3.6.2 Negligent advice and negligent misstatement

As we have already seen, depending on the practitioner's particular therapeutic approach and modality, advice giving may sometimes form an essential part of therapy (e.g. recommendations for homework) and sometimes it may not. A claim in contract or in tort may arise in respect of an economic loss allegedly resulting from acting upon advice or information that has been given negligently by a therapist, but usually claims in tort for negligent advice or negligent misstatement are brought against solicitors, financial advisers, or bankers – see the leading case of *Hedley Byrne & Co Ltd* v *Heller & Partners Ltd* [1963] 3 WLR 101, [1964] AC 465.

If we apply the general principles laid down by the House of Lords in *Hedley Byrne*, as subsequently developed, to a theoretical claim against a therapist, in order to succeed the claimant would have to prove, among other things, that:

- the negligent advice was given in the course of therapy by a therapist with (or claiming) special skill or knowledge
- the therapist took responsibility for the advice given
- the therapist owed a duty of care to the claimant
- it was reasonably foreseeable that the client would act upon that advice
- no disclaimer was given at the time
- the client's subsequent acting upon the advice caused an economic loss.

As a result of the line of cases following *Hedley Byrne*, many bankers, surveyors and other professionals issue disclaimers of liability when proffering their advice and/or ensure effective cover for advice with professional indemnity insurance. Therapists who give advice as part of their therapy will need to consider the potential ethical and legal impact of advice giving, and the impact of a disclaimer on the therapeutic alliance. Effective professional indemnity insurance cover serves to protect both therapist and client.

3.6.3 Vicarious liability

An employer may be held liable for the actions of an employee when that employee is acting in the course of their duty as an employee. For example, a bank, solicitors' or accountants' firm may be held liable for the actions of their employees acting in the course of their employment, and they hold professional liability insurance to cover their staff. An agency, company or organisation employing therapists may in the same way be held liable to clients for the actions of each employed counsellor acting in the course of their employment. The individual professional insurance of the counsellors may not therefore protect the firm itself. See Chapter 6 for further discussion of insurance matters and Chapter 9 for employment.

3.6.4 Contributory negligence and voluntary assumption of risk

A client who makes a claim against their therapist may have exacerbated the loss that they allege resulted from the therapist's negligence, by their own actions. This is 'contributory negligence'. In a claim for damages made against the therapist, any proven contributory negligence on the part of the client may significantly reduce any damages which might be awarded to a successful claimant.

If a claimant is proved to have voluntarily assumed a risk, this too may reduce their damages. For example, the person who gets into a car driven by a driver whom they know to have been drinking may have their damages proportionately reduced in the event of a claim following a car crash.

It is just possible to envisage circumstances where, should a client allege that damage has been caused by therapy, contributory negligence might also become a factor in the issues considered by the court. However, therapeutic codes of practice (the 'soft law', including government guidelines) strongly support ethical duty to vulnerable clients, creating a protective environment for clients. Balanced against this is the legal difficulty for clients in holding therapists accountable for the outcome of events in their life – therapists usually agree in their therapeutic contract that they are responsible *to* clients, and not *for* clients, who remain in charge of their own lives.

3.7 What is the standard of care expected of a therapist?

An ordinary person (traditionally defined by lawyers from an old case as 'the man on the Clapham omnibus') needs to take an ordinary level of care in what they do in their daily life, e.g. driving. Therapists are ordinary people in their daily life, and professionals when at work. Professionals in their field are expected to exercise higher standards of skills in their work than ordinary individuals when undertaking their specialist activities. For example, a therapist should take ordinary care when driving home from work, but a higher level of care when working therapeutically with clients or supervisees, writing reports or making referrals, etc.

It is difficult to define or describe with precision the legal standards of care and skill that might be expected of a therapist in the UK because of the dearth of relevant cases against therapists. We are probably relieved that there have been so few cases against therapists so far, but it means that we are thrown back to the ethical frameworks of our professional organisations for guidance on standards, rather than looking to the courts for answers. As seen in Chapter 1, government guidance increasingly impacts on therapeutic practice.

However, we can perhaps deduce certain standards from cases on medical negligence. Even here, the courts have difficulty where some professionals differ in opinion as to what is right. As Lord President Clyde put it in the case of *Hunter* v *Hanley* [1955] SC 204: 'In the realm of diagnosis and treatment there is ample scope for genuine differences of professional opinion and one man clearly is not negligent merely because his conclusion differs from that of other professional men.'

The general standard of care expected of competent professionals (now called the '*Bolam* test') was first established in the negligence case of *Bolam* v *Friern Hospital Management Committee* [1957] 2 All ER 118, [1957] 1 WLR 582. This case concerned the administration of electro-convulsive therapy (ECT) to a patient without anaesthetic or any muscle relaxant drugs, and he sustained serious spinal injury as a result. Although this would, hopefully, never happen today, the treatment reflected accepted medical practice at that time, and the doctor concerned was not found to be negligent. McNair J (at p. 587) described the level of skill required:

> The test is that of the ordinary skilled man exercising and professing to have that skill. A man need not possess the highest expert skill; it is well established law that it is sufficient if he exercises the ordinary skill of an ordinary competent man exercising that particular art.

In the context of the '*Bolam* test', it is probable, however, that a highly specialised person (an expert) practising in a particular professional field would be expected by the courts to exercise a higher standard of care than the ordinary practitioner who does not have the benefit of that expert's extra training and experience: 'In the case of specialists, it is likely that the standard of care would be that of 'reasonably competent members of the profession who have the same rank and profess the same specialisation, if any as the defendant' (see Powers and Harris 2000: 1.58, in Oliphant, 2007: 751).

The House of Lords approved the *Bolam* test (see *Sidaway* v *Governors of Bethlem Royal Hospital* [1985] AC 871 at 897) and it stood unchallenged for 40 years, but it was modified in the case of *Bolitho* v *City of Hackney Health Authority* [1997] AC 232, [1997] 4 All ER 771. This was a case of a small boy who was admitted to hospital and who suffered brain damage in hospital while an in-patient. The issue was whether his medical treatment had been negligent. Until this case, the *Bolam* test had allowed compliance with accepted medical practice as a defence. In other words, until then, the medical profession, rather than the courts, had been dictating the standard of care.

The *Bolitho* case qualified this. The courts accept that a reasonable expert medical opinion will involve balancing the risks and benefits of treatment, and is a matter for clinical judgement, but as most judges are not medically qualified, they need expert evidence to help them. In the *Bolitho* case, the judges held that experts should be expected to give the reasons for their opinion, which could then be assessed by the court with reference to logic and common sense. If, in future negligence cases, there are two conflicting bodies of expert opinion, and in the court's view one of them is not supported by logic, then the court may reject that opinion as a benchmark for the standard of care.

In the case of therapy, the opinions sought might be those of the therapist's professional organisation, or those of respected colleagues with equal or higher qualifications and experience. For members of the BACP, for example, reference may be made to accepted practice in compliance with the *Ethical Framework* (BACP 2010).

The standard of care in Scotland

The test for professional negligence in Scotland has its foundations in the *Hunter* v *Hanley* case, referred to above. This case involved a doctor, but it is accepted as applying to general questions of professional negligence, and its applicability is not confined to medicine. In a therapy situation, based on the opinion of the court in *Hunter* v *Hanley*, the test for negligence in Scots law can be outlined as follows:

1. There was a normal practice adopted by therapists in the situation in which the treating therapist in the particular case found themselves.
2. This 'normal practice', or approach to treatment of the patient, was not followed in the particular case.
3. This deviation from the normal practice was not one which any therapist, acting with due skill and care, would have adopted.

As with the position in the English courts, whether the above criteria have been met will usually only be capable of being determined by a court after hearing expert evidence from other therapists – whether they are able to speak of the presence or absence of a normal practice in a particular treatment scenario and, where there has been a departure from a normal practice, the reasonableness of that departure. On the basis of the criteria above, a therapist practising in Scotland is extremely unlikely to be found to have been negligent by a court unless evidence shows that no ordinarily competent therapist, acting with due skill and care, would have taken the same course of action.

3.7.1 Continuing professional development

Working to a professional standard of care includes an implied duty on professionals to keep up to date with developments in practice. Those working in the health care professions are regulated by the Health Act 1999, implemented by the Commission for Health Care Audit and Inspection (CHI). In non-NHS settings, counselling and psychotherapy are not yet regulated (although this is predicted for 2012) but many professional counselling and psychotherapy organisations impose continuing professional development (CPD) as part of the conditions of membership, e.g. BACP (2009), BPS and UKCP.

3.7.2 The National Institute for Health and Clinical Excellence (NICE) guidelines

Sir Michael Rawlins (Chairman of the National Institute of Clinical Excellence (NICE)) said that 'NICE guidelines are likely to constitute a responsible body of medical opinion for the purposes of litigation. … Doctors are advised to record their reasons for deviating from the guidelines' (Rawlins 2003). NICE provides guidelines for therapy, which are recommendations for the treatment for specified mental conditions, e.g. post-traumatic stress disorder (PTSD), depression and anxiety, and they influence referrals and treatment programmes offered within the NHS.

Although many therapists do not work within the NHS, should a legal case be brought against them for negligence, we think that (given the *Bolam* test as amended by *Bolitho* described in 3.7 above) any failure to comply with the NICE guidelines would have to be explained and justified, since the NICE guidelines are part of the 'soft law' mentioned in the Introduction.

Many therapists may question the rationale by which the NICE guidelines were developed and set. For example, some have questioned the use of the research which underpins the current recommendations about preferred treatment modalities in psychological therapy. However, the influence of the NICE guidelines within the NHS may influence the courts' perceptions of therapy outside the NHS, and the perceived need to comply with or explain departure from them may pose potential problems for any therapists against whom a negligence case is brought, whose approach is not one of the recommended treatment modalities for a specific issue (e.g. anxiety, depression, PTSD).

3.8 How is a duty of care and negligence proved?

The claimant has to prove in court that a duty of care existed and that the defendant breached it by negligence (falling below the appropriate standard of care), causing some sort of damage. It is usually said the case must be proved 'upon a balance of probabilities' (i.e. that it is more likely than not) that the events occurred as the claimant alleges. That statement is a little simplistic because sometimes the standard of proof will vary depending on the circumstances (see *Pettenden* [1988] 7CQJ 220), and the more grave the allegation, or the more serious the nature of the allegations, a higher burden of proof may be necessary (*Hornal* v *Neuberger Products Ltd* [1957] 1 QB 247).

Note that, by contrast, the burden of proof in criminal cases is much tougher – the prosecution in criminal cases must satisfy the court of the defendant's guilt 'beyond reasonable doubt'.

3.9 Can a third party (e.g. a member of the client's family) sue the therapist for negligence?

Actions by third parties such as relatives are rare. This is because a third party would need to prove a contractual liability, or vicarious liability (for example, an employer may be liable for the actions of their employee in the course of their work), or that they were in some way entitled to act on behalf of the claimant or their estate, such as where the claimant is mentally incapacitated or is a child. By analogy with medical cases, the relatives of a deceased client may have a cause of action provided that the other factors in negligence (see 3.6) or contract are proved to have been met. However, just as there are very few cases against therapists, there are even fewer cases brought against therapists by third parties. The reason for this is the difficulty usually encountered by third parties in proving the legal chain of causation linking the essential elements of the case: the duty of care, the person responsible, and the negligent act or omission, as a clear cause of the damage suffered.

One example of a risk for which a third party might sue a therapist is where someone has not been warned of danger from a potentially violent client and is then harmed. In the UK, at the moment, the law does not impose a general duty on a therapist to warn others of impending danger from a client. When thinking of those who may be in danger, there is a distinction between those whom the client may have specifically named as potential victims and others who might be identifiable with some research (e.g. the client's friends, relatives, etc.). In the UK there is no specific statutory duty to warn either group, or to report crime, save in certain exceptional circumstances, such as terrorism. However, a therapist who is concerned for the safety of a client or of others may breach confidentiality with the consent of the client or, in the absence of consent, the therapist may use their discretion to breach confidentiality to prevent a serious crime, or to prevent harm to the client or vulnerable others. For a detailed list, see Table 3.2 below. In such cases, although the client may object to the disclosure and seek to prevent it or to obtain redress afterwards, the courts would tend to uphold the disclosure if it is in the public interest (and therefore not award damages against the therapist for breach of confidentiality) because the public interest would outweigh the contractual duty of confidentiality (see the case of *W* v *Egdell*). We have discussed these complex issues in detail in *Confidentiality and Record Keeping in Counselling and Psychotherapy* (Bond and Mitchels 2008), and also in the BACP Information Sheet G2, *Breaches in Confidentiality* (Bond et al. 2008).

There is a potentially complex situation where a therapist works with couples and families. Here, the therapeutic contract is likely to be with more than one

Table 3.2   Deciding whether to breach confidentiality to prevent clients harming others

Situation	Breaching confidentiality	Legal authorities
Preventing or assisting the detection of terrorism	There is a duty to disclose specified types of information acquired in the course of a trade, profession, business or employment: see Chapter 3.	Section 19 and s 38B of the Terrorism Act 2000.
Preventing or assisting detection of drug trafficking and money laundering	Respond in the same way as for any serious crime. Requirements to report, which included therapists in the past, have largely been replaced in current UK legislation: see Chapter 3.	Drug Trafficking Act 1994. Proceeds of Crime Act 2002.
Prevention of serious crime	Permissible at discretion of therapist acting in good faith to notify authorities.	In common law, the public interest in the prevention and detection of serious crime is greater than in protecting confidences.
	A court is unlikely to impose any penalties for breach of confidence that is considered to be in the public interest. Such breaches are 'defensible'.	Balance of public interest in common law.
	A client cannot insist on confidentiality over serious crime.	Law of equity under the principle that 'there is no confidence in iniquity'.
Prevention of serious physical harm likely to be inflicted by client on another adult	A breach of confidence is defensible in order to protect someone from serious physical harm inflicted by a client where the information is given in good faith, reasonably well founded, restricted to that necessary to prevent the harm, and communicated in confidence to either the authorities or the intended victim.	Common law – balance of public interest. Where a client is likely to harm another of the therapist's clients, failure to act to protect the victim may amount to negligence. Legal advice should be sought if circumstances permit this. In an emergency situation, it may be better to avert a serious and real risk of harm by warning the potential victim, if they are unaware of the danger, or informing police to prevent immediate injury. This type of dilemma may arise when providing couple counselling while also working with one of them individually.

Situation	Breaching confidentiality	Legal authorities
		The ethical issues are increased when seeing a client who is intending to inflict harm on another person who is also your client, without one or both clients knowing that the other is receiving therapy from you. Consider issues in the checklists on pages 126–7.
Prevention of psychological harm likely to be inflicted by client on another adult	No general grounds to breach confidentiality.	Common law balance of public interest requires prevention of serious *physical* harm. However, the law is moving towards taking substantial psychological harm more seriously, especially if this harm amounts to psychiatric illness or is being inflicted on a vulnerable adult. The law provides protection against stalking, harassment and discrimination in many circumstances but it is less clear whether these situations would justify a breach of confidence. Work with the client's consent or seek legal advice.
Knowledge of significant harm being caused or likely to be caused to a child/young person		
Prevention of serious physical harm being inflicted by client on self, whether life threatening or not, *that places others at risk of serious physical harm*	Respond as though for prevention of serious crime where crime might result, or on the balance of public interest to prevent serious physical harm to others.	Balance of public interest. Consider the issues in the Disclosure Checklist (p. 127).
Prevention of self-inflicted serious physical harm to an adult client	May be defensible to consult a medic or specialist in mental health on a confidential basis to investigate the possibility of compulsory assessment or treatment *where mental illness is suspected.*	No case law could be discovered but may be defensible on the balance of public interest – depending on the circumstances. Consider the issues in the Disclosure Checklist (p. 127).
	If the client explicitly refuses permission to seek medical assistance for the treatment of physical injuries.	Check that client has mental capacity. No general right to breach confidentiality against the express wishes of the client. Persuasion to

(Continued)

Table 3.2   (Continued)

Situation	Breaching confidentiality	Legal authorities
		accept help is legally safer. Adults with mental capacity may refuse treatments for physical illnesses or offers of assistance even if it seems contrary to their best interests or unreasonable. (*St George's Healthcare NHS Trust v S* [1999])
Prevention of self-inflicted serious physical harm by someone under the age of 18	There is no general legal requirement to breach confidentiality but therapists working in public authorities or associated organisations may be obliged to do so under child protection law and their contract of employment. All therapists should comply with child protection law.	The public policy and the balance of public interest in common law favours ensuring that children are protected and therefore would protect a breach of confidence, even against the young person's express wishes to obtain assistance or advice. Consider the issues in the checklists on pages 126–7.
Seeking treatment for minor or superficial self-inflicted harm by someone between 16 and 18 years old	The express wishes of the person concerned should normally be respected, however, mental capacity should be carefully considered along with the issues in the Disclosure Checklist (p. 127).	Family Law Reform Act 1969; Age of Legal Capacity (Scotland) Act 1991.
Seeking treatment for minor or superficial self-inflicted harm by someone under 16	The express wishes of someone who is 'Gillick competent' i.e. having sufficient age, intelligence and understanding to understand the consequences of declining treatment should normally be respected. However, consider the issues in the Disclosure Checklist (p. 127).	*Gillick v West Norfolk and Wisbech Area Health Authority* [1985]; Age of Legal Capacity (Scotland) Act 1991.
	Where someone lacks the mental capacity to give consent, consider seeking the involvement and consent of someone with parental responsibility. (One person's consent is sufficient if there is more than one person with parental responsibility.) Whilst the young person's wishes and feelings should be taken into account, their welfare should be paramount and guide any further action.	Lord Fraser's judgment in Gillick case (see above).

person, each of whom is a client, and each person is therefore owed a duty of care, both in contract law and as a general duty in the law of negligence. The duty of care to one person in the couple or family does not eclipse the duty of care owed to the other(s).

The therapeutic contract should ideally reflect a mutual agreement about sharing information with the other client or family members (or making referrals) if there is a risk of serious harm. In the absence of such a clear contractual agreement, if there should be an imminent risk of serious harm to one of the couple or a member of their family, it is our view that the general duty of care may require giving an appropriate warning. If challenged in the courts, such a warning is likely to be considered fully justifiable in the public interest.

In the USA, in the case of *Tarasoff* v *Regents of the University of California* [1976] Sup. Ct. Cal. [1976]; 551 P 2d 334, the courts faced exactly this dilemma. A young and highly disturbed man was infatuated with Tatania Tarasoff, a student at the University of California. He threatened to kill her and obtained a gun. He was receiving psychotherapy and told his therapist about his intention. The therapist told the police, and tried to have the young man compulsorily detained. However, the therapist did not warn the girl herself or her parents. She was killed by the student two months later. The parents sued the university, holding them vicariously liable as the employer of the therapist for his negligence. The Supreme Court in California found that there existed a duty to warn identifiable third parties of risk from a dangerous patient, and a concomitant legal liability in clinical negligence for failure to do so, with damages payable to the party or, as in this case, to the deceased person's estate. In Michigan, USA in 1983, this liability was confirmed and further extended to cover non-identifiable third parties (i.e. a duty to issue a general warning) – see *Davies* v *LHIM* (1983) 335 NW 2d 481 Michigan Supreme Court.

As a result of these cases, some academics and lawyers (see, for example, Turner and Kennedy 2008) may feel that there is a growing sense within the profession that warning third parties, after weighing up the possible negative consequences to the patients of taking such a step, is becoming more a requirement of 'soft law' than simply appropriate professional behaviour, but it leaves many unanswered dilemmas as to how and when such warnings would be appropriate.

On the issue of liability of third parties, in 2003, the Chief Medical Officer, Professor Sir Liam Donaldson, published *Making Amends*, a key consultation report into clinical negligence in the NHS (Donaldson 2003). In it he set out proposals to fundamentally reform the way clinical negligence cases are handled in the health service, including the establishment of an NHS Redress Scheme to speed up the process and offer care and compensation under certain circumstances without the necessity to go to court. A Clinical Negligence Scheme was then set up by the NHS. The full version of the report is available on the Department of Health website at: www.doh.gov.uk/makingamends. See also the

National Health Service (Clinical Negligence Scheme) Amendment (No. 2) 2006 for liability to third parties.

3.10 Supervision – responsibility and liability to supervisees and their clients

As we have seen in Chapter 2 at 2.4, the respective duties of the supervisor and supervisee will depend in part on their professional modality, their contract of supervision, and the organisational setting within which they work. In some organisations, supervisors have both managerial and supervisory relationship, with their supervisees. Where there is a management responsibility, there is also likely to be an employment or other contractual relationship – for further discussion see Chapters 4 and 9.

The focus of supervision is necessarily on the needs and interests of the supervisee's clients (Page and Wosket 1998). Information sharing between professionals appropriately is essential here and good professional practice necessitates the supervisee being honest and open in bringing difficulties in their work to supervision (see Bond 1990; Bond and Mitchels 2008: chapters 5 and 9).

A supervisor is contractually bound and has ethical responsibility to the supervisee, but has no direct contractual relationship with the supervisee's client(s). The supervisor does, however, owe an ethical duty to the supervisee's clients to provide competent professional oversight of the supervisee's practice for their benefit. The supervisor may have to give authoritative action or advice about best practice when a client is at risk and a supervisee needs guidance or direction (Page and Wosket 1998: 22).

In theory, therefore, in the law of tort, a supervisor could potentially be held liable in the context of their role in relation to a client who has been brought to supervision and in respect of whom the supervisor had provided bad advice and guidance which was then acted upon by the supervisee to the detriment of the client. Such a claim would be difficult to bring because it would depend upon proof of a chain of legal causation linking the supervisor's advice with any relevant subsequent actions by the supervisee, and again linking those actions directly with any resulting damage to the client. A complicating factor is that there may be somewhere along this chain the actions of the claimant or other individuals which may have contributed to the cause or exacerbated the damage or loss. The chain is, for all these reasons, likely to be tenuous and difficult to establish in law.

As we pointed out in Chapter 2, we are not aware of any claim of this sort brought against a supervisor in England and Wales, and of course in situations such as peer group supervision, in which the advice given (and therefore the legal responsibility for it) may be collectively shared, legal responsibility would be even more difficult to establish. However, society is becoming more litigious and there is always a first time for any type of legal action!

We are aware of a complaint made by a client in which a supervisor was brought into the disciplinary procedure by the counsellor's professional organisation. The organisation needed to ascertain the precise nature of information shared, advice given and to discuss ethical duties. In any legal case brought which alleges the professional negligence of a supervisor, legal advice should be sought on the specific circumstances of that case. For further discussion of relevant issues see Chapter 4 (Contract), Chapter 6 (Insurance) and Chapter 9 (Employment).

Many professional organisations (e.g. BACP) may require reports from a supervisor for accreditation, registration, fellowship or disciplinary purposes. In all these situations, the supervisor is legally responsible to the supervisee and to the organisation concerned for the accuracy and professional competency of their reports. Supervisors should be careful to include in reports any relevant information given to them by others on which their advice/opinion was based, and also to clarify the source, rather than presenting facts as their own.

3.11 Should I apologise? If I do apologise, will it damage my case?

It seems that some car drivers are advised by their insurance companies not to apologise after an accident in case this is taken as an admission of guilt or fault. As therapists, we may not like this advice since we may naturally feel for and with our clients, and even when they are complaining about us, we may (despite feeling that we acted rightly) still empathise with that client's situation or needs. The law has now been clarified by s. 2 of the Compensation Act 2006, which provides that: 'An apology, an offer of treatment or other redress, shall not of itself amount to an admission of negligence or a breach of statutory duty.' Let's hope that the courts continue to use sound common sense and interpret events in the spirit of the Compensation Act.

Therapists practising in Scotland should bear in mind that s. 2 of the Compensation Act 2006 does not apply in Scotland.

3.12 How can I protect myself from claims for negligence?

No therapist can ever be totally 'bullet proof' against complaints and legal claims for negligence, since clients may at any time decide to complain or litigate about any aspect of their therapy. However, there is a substantial measure of protection against spurious complaints and actions in the disciplinary procedures operated by the professional organisations, and also by the legal system and court procedures.

Complaints and court claims received must be properly presented, in due form, and then they will be assessed. There will be a rejection by professional bodies of complaints (or claims) which are maliciously made, unsubstantiated by cogent evidence, or which do not otherwise show that the therapist has fallen below a reasonable standard of professional practice. In the case of court cases for negligence, as seen earlier in this chapter, the courts require a clear chain of proof of both negligence and causation, i.e. proof that the actions or omissions of the therapist fell below a reasonable standard to be expected and caused damage to the client which could be compensated financially or by injunction.

a)   Therapists should ensure, as far as possible, that their work is always carried out to a reasonable professional standard

Maintaining professional standards can be achieved in a variety of ways:

*   Belonging to and working within the codes of ethics and conduct of a reputable professional organisation appropriate for the therapist's chosen modality (or modalities). Some organisations, such as BACP, cover a wide range of modalities. Others may have a membership drawn from a narrower range of modalities (e.g. UKCP).
*   Making effective and appropriate use of supervision with a competent and experienced supervisor who is familiar with the therapist's chosen modality (or modalities).
*   Continuing professional development through training courses and reading.
*   Participation in peer activities, e.g. workshops, conferences and networking.
*   Keeping up to date with developments in practice through journals, research, networking, etc.

(b)   Before therapy begins, make an assessment of the client's needs in the context of their background and circumstances, including a clear understanding of the client's hopes and expectations of therapy

Effective and thorough assessment can underpin and inform the therapeutic contract, and be useful to both therapist and the client in choosing the appropriate modality, form and possible duration (and therefore possibly also the potential cost) of therapy (see BACP Information Sheet P13, *Assessment in Counselling and Psychotherapy* (Tasker 2008)).

Some complaints may arise from clients who feel that they have not been 'cured' as they had hoped. They may have had unreal expectations of therapy or of themselves, and/or the therapist may not have had the necessary skill to address the client's issues appropriately. Bear in mind that our assessment as therapists of whether we have the requisite professional expertise must always be considered in relation to the needs of each individual client. Supervision, or other expert advice, can assist therapists to make this evaluation where there is any doubt.

(c)   Do not take on clients who have needs that cannot be met in therapy with you. Consider referral where appropriate and necessary

(d)   Create clarity of mutual expectations with clients at the outset of the work and reflect it in a therapeutic contract

Assessment can identify the needs, hopes and expectations of the client. Following on from this, the discussion, negotiation and agreement of the therapeutic contract is vitally important (see Chapter 4 and BACP Information Sheet P11, *Making the Contract for Counselling and Psychotherapy* (Dale 2008a).

(e)   Beware of making extravagant promises and predicting outcomes

Be very cautious about predicting outcomes to the client. Therapists should be realistic and pragmatic, remembering that responsibility for the outcome of therapy depends largely on the client, who will come to be known and understood better during the course of therapy. So, to avoid claims for misrepresentation or breach of contract, it is most unwise to make extravagant claims for therapy and, as Cohen (1992) says '…the wisest of them promise nothing at all!' (Bond 2009: 70).

Finally, we cannot emphasise too strongly that this chapter can give only a general outline of relevant legal issues, and is therefore not legal advice, because the law has to be applied to the specific circumstances of each situation. Each therapist and client has their own particular therapeutic alliance, so wherever a therapist needs clarification of an issue of law, it is important to seek specialist legal advice on the particular circumstances of the case.

4 Contracts

Is there a difference between an agreement and a contract?

What makes a legal contract?

As a therapist, this year I signed an employment contract with a counselling agency, an insurance agreement, a contract for room hire for my private work, and yet another for supervision. Are all these contracts governed by the same legal rules?

I never know what to put into a therapeutic contract. There is so much to think about, sometimes I just wonder … 'What could I safely leave out?'

Should I offer all my clients a standard contract with the same terms or make different therapeutic contracts to suit each client?

Do we have to put the therapeutic contract in writing? That all seems so formal somehow …

Do clients have duties under therapeutic contracts as well as us?

I am a trainee, with a supervisor who, I am told, also has some responsibilities to my training organisation. It is all so complicated. Who is actually under a contract, and who with and for what?

If I allow a spouse, partner or family member to attend a session with my client, what contractual rights might they have?

Once I have made a contract with a client, can one of us ever get out of it? How should we do it?

If a client claimed that I had broken our therapeutic contract, what could happen to me?

We frequently mention contracts in various contexts: at work, perhaps employment or therapeutic contracts; at home, possibly in relation to buying, leasing or renting a home, insurance, loans and mortgages, telephone, internet or fuel supply; in our general personal and family living, e.g. legal, financial and other professional advice; and leisure activities, such as joining a gym or booking a holiday. Few of us stop to consider in detail what we actually mean by the term, what actually makes a contract that is legally enforceable. This chapter takes a look at the legal aspects of making, keeping and sometimes breaching contracts, different types of contractual agreements, and the remedies available for breach of the different types of contract. We are not trying here to turn readers into lawyers, but simply provide a road map through 'the thickets of the law' to make some common sense of it all and to indicate the potential problem areas. Contract is varied and situation-specific, and if one is in any doubt about a particular contract, legal advice should be sought.

4.1 What is a contract?

4.1.1 Comparing contracts and agreements

Contracts are fairly easy to recognise, once you know what you are looking for, but very difficult to define. They are legally enforceable agreements, usually regulating the sale, lease or transfer of land, or the provision of goods, advice or services for an agreed price. Contracts can therefore vary widely, but a good legally enforceable contract is rather like a 'nut roast' (a vegetarian dish with infinite varieties, but traditionally made from a mixture of nuts, a bulking ingredient, flavouring, and something that sticks the whole thing together), because although there is no single recipe, each one can be successfully made by following certain principles.

Legally enforceable contracts embody a number of essential ingredients which may be explicit or implied:

- a promise (e.g. to do or supply something)
- an agreement, and
- an exchange (e.g. of money in return for goods or services).

Since the nineteenth century, these essential ingredients have been defined and analysed by the courts in contract law as 'offer', 'acceptance' and 'consideration' (these terms are explored in further detail in 4.1.2).

In Scotland, the courts recognise a further requirement for the formation of a binding contract: *consensus ad idem*. This requires that parties have reached a mutual understanding and agreement about the terms of the contract. This is tested objectively rather than subjectively. An example of a situation where there might not be *consensus ad idem* would be if one party thought that a contract was for hire, and one thought that it was for purchase. In England and Wales, this concept underpins and is reflected in contract law, for example the need for clarity in offer and acceptance, and in the law relating to mistake, explored below.

Sometimes, the terms of a contract are not explicitly stated by the parties each time, but are implied in common law. For example, when buying petrol for the car, it is possible that no words are spoken at all while the driver fills up the car, goes to the kiosk, proffers money in payment and receives a receipt. Nevertheless, there is a contract in which the parties expect the petrol to be of a certain quality and delivered in the right amount, and that the driver will pay the appropriate money in exchange. The terms of the contract can be clearly understood by the parties because the type and quality of the petrol, the exact amount delivered and the price payable should all be clearly visible at the garage.

In counselling, the expectations may not be so well implied or understood by both parties. When clients arrive for the first time, they do not always have a clear idea of what they expect or want from the therapy, they may be unaware of the rates charged or whether they have to pay for missed sessions, or what to do if they are not satisfied with the progress of their therapy. The therapist herself may not have considered what to do about missed sessions or late payments. Client and therapist may have different expectations about confidentiality. Some of these potential contractual terms can be clarified by the provision of a leaflet for the client to read in advance, setting out the basic terms of the therapy offered, or by careful discussion with new clients at their intake assessment or first session. Be careful if relying on verbal contracts reached at the first therapeutic session. Clients may be anxious and not concentrating, and so are less able to reach a considered agreement with the therapist, or they may fail to recall what was agreed. Better, in our view, to have a written therapeutic contract for clarity and as an *aide-mémoire*.

4.1.2 What makes a contract legally enforceable? 'Offer', 'acceptance', 'consideration' and capacity

The courts adjudicate on a wide variety of contracts, and to facilitate the decision-making process, they gradually developed a system of analysis of common contract features, in which the 'promisor' (or 'offeror') promises or offers to do something, in return for which the 'promisee' (or 'offeree') agrees to provide, do, or not do something in return (the 'consideration'). For example, a therapist may offer to provide therapy in return for which the client agrees to provide money payment, or two therapist colleagues may agree to provide each other with peer supervision, for which neither ask for payment.

Robert Bradgate (2007: 236–7) explains that the questions that the courts have to answer in considering whether a legally binding contract exists are as follows:

- Was there a definite promise?
- Was it intended to be binding?
- Was it supported by consideration so as to make it binding?

The courts will look at the facts of each contract objectively and infer an intention to be legally bound, provided that the agreement was expressed in sufficiently clear language, defining the promise made and the consideration to be given, and therefore the court can conclude that a reasonable person in the position of the parties would consider themselves legally bound to fulfil the agreement.

Offer and acceptance

The parties to a contract must first reach a mutual understanding of the precise scope and terms of their agreement. The offeror must have made an unequivocal promise to the offeree, who unequivocally and unconditionally accepts it. Robert Bradgate puts it very well:

An offer is any statement which indicates that the person making it is willing to undertake a legal obligation if the terms it contains are satisfied by the person to whom it is made doing something, or undertaking to do or forbear from doing something, in return. An acceptance is a statement made in response to an offer which indicates that the person making it, to whom the offer was made, agrees without qualification to all of the terms proposed by the offeror.

(Bradgate 2007: 387)

As an example, a therapist or agency may advertise, but the provision of therapy may be subject to certain conditions (e.g. assessment for suitability, payment, etc.), and so assessment and negotiation may be necessary before entering into a therapeutic contract.

In a shop, when the intending purchaser takes the goods to the checkout till and/or approaches a sales assistant and requests to buy them, it is at this point that the terms of sale are clarified (e.g. the purchase price, guarantees, delivery date, etc.) and this is the 'offer'. The purchaser could at this stage change their mind and back away from making the purchase. The shopkeeper could also withdraw the offer and refuse to make the sale. In the same way, once the therapist explains the terms of therapy, a client may discuss and consider their options, and they or the therapist may decide not to enter into a therapeutic contract.

The customer's agreement to buy the goods is the acceptance. When the goods are handed over or delivered and the money promised by the customer in return (the consideration) is paid, the contract is then fulfilled. When therapy is provided, there is an obligation on the part of the client to fulfil their part of the contract, and to make any payment that has been agreed.

In the case of a self-service supermarket with a fully automatic checkout, the offer and acceptance both happen when the customer goes to the checkout till and begins the process of checking the items through the till. Common law will imply that the customer is willing to pay the price displayed on the chosen goods, and the contract is complete when the payment is made (consideration given) and the goods taken by the customer. This kind of situation is less comparable with therapy, which involves a professional relationship, but in situations where agencies provide advance written information with clear conditions and terms of their service, and a client indicates that they have read and understood those conditions, attends for sessions and pays in accordance with the terms, a contract might be inferred. For ethical and legal reasons, however, we would advise that therapists openly discuss and agree the terms of their service with their clients in advance of the provision of therapy, and that for the avoidance of doubt, the agreement is reflected in writing.

Consideration

The modern law concerning consideration is complex, having developed from the old case of *Eastwood* v *Kenyon* [1840] 11 Ad & El 438. In essence, consideration might be thought of as 'the price of a promise' *Dunlop* v *Selfridge* [1915] AC 847 at 855 per Lord Dunedin.

Some promises are made with no requirement of consideration. They may be legally enforceable if they are written down and signed, witnessed and delivered as a formal legal deed (e.g. the gift of land to a relative), but they are different from the simple contracts supported by consideration. An example of such a legal deed would be a document which is drafted, signed and witnessed in compliance with s. 1 of the Law of Property (Miscellaneous Provisions) Act 1989, or is made by a limited company, under s 36A of the Companies Act 1985. The most important practical use of deeds in this way is to avoid the need for consideration when the promisor wishes to make a gratuitous promise binding, e.g. a gift to charity or a voluntary agreement by a creditor to release a debt.

In private practice, therapy is frequently provided in return for payment. The fee structure for therapy should be discussed and agreed before the work begins (e.g. the hourly fee, session duration, frequency, and length of therapy) so that the client knows clearly in advance so far as is possible how much they will have to pay.

What if we forget to agree the fees?

If the fees are not clarified and agreed in advance of providing therapy, the parties have no clear legally enforceable contract because the terms are not yet settled. There are also potential ethical issues here, for example concerning failure to support client autonomy and possible lack of self-respect for the therapist (BACP 2009). If the client then receives therapy but fails to pay any fee, the therapist may have difficulty in enforcing payment. If this should happen, once a therapist realises their mistake and wishes to continue working with that client, they should discuss and negotiate the terms of the therapy as soon as possible for an effective contract to be established, at least for their future work.

There is an old established rule that if A does work for B, at B's request, in circumstances where *both* parties would reasonably expect A to be paid for it, and B then promises to pay a particular sum for that work, then B's promise would be enforceable (see *Lampleigh* v *Braithwait* [1615] Hob 105). In Scotland, a similar rule, *quantum meruit*, applies. These rules might rescue the situation if the client is willing to pay a reasonable fee, but prevention is far better than cure. Most therapists would not want to have to take a client to court to obtain payment for past sessions.

Can there still be a contract if therapy is provided free of charge?

In the case of therapy given for payment, the existence of a legally binding contract may be clearer than in other situations where therapy is provided entirely free of any direct charge to the client, e.g. by a volunteer therapist working with a charitable agency, or by a therapist working in an NHS general practitioner (GP) surgery or a hospital. In all situations, the therapist should act with a professional duty of care (see Chapter 3 on negligence), and therapists working within the NHS have to abide by their specific government agency rules and guidance. A contract between the client and the NHS may be inferred because the NHS provides services to the public in return for public contributions in taxation. Heath care may then be provided by the therapist as an employee or agent of the NHS.

The legal position of a private therapy practitioner working in a GP surgery will depend upon that particular therapist's contract with the GP service (see Chapter 9 for employer/employee and agency relationships).

An interesting case is that of *Gore* v *Van der Lann* [1967] 2QB 31, [1967] 1 All ER 360, in which a pensioner had a free bus pass, so expected to travel without payment. This was held to be an enforceable contract because, although Gore had no prior relationship with the bus company, he had to fill in an application form to claim his pass. The consideration was the filling in of the form. Based on *Gore*, one wonders if, provided that both parties intend the relationship to be contractual, in situations where therapy is provided free, the courts might hold that there is a legally binding therapeutic contract if the client has had to do something to obtain the service, e.g. filling in a form, attending the counselling sessions regularly, etc.

In order to enter into a valid contract, the parties must have mental capacity. For adults, mental capacity is now governed by the Mental Capacity Act 2005. For minors, the relevant law is s. 1 of the Family Law Reform Act 1969, which lowered the age of majority from 21 to 18, and the Minors' Contracts Act 1987, which allows minors (children and young people under the age of 18) to go back on contracts, with some exceptions. Mental capacity and the ability of minors and vulnerable adults to enter into contracts are discussed in this chapter at 4.6 and 4.7.

4.1.3 Should contracts be in writing?

Some contracts, for example for the sale or lease of land, must be 'evidenced in writing' to be legally enforceable (Law of Property Act 1925, s. 52). It is therefore advisable to ensure that all agreements for a lease or tenancy of premises and sales of land are in writing. It is advisable to obtain legal advice for sales of land and purchasing leases and tenancies because there are often complex legal and financial issues involved and pitfalls to be avoided, particularly in this current climate of rapid changes in property values.

There are some specific statutory requirements for certain types of contract to be written or evidenced in writing, including contracts for employment (see Chapter 9), insurance (see Chapter 6), guarantees, hire, consumer credit, and for the sale of certain specified goods and services.

Other contracts for the sale of services (such as therapy) may be verbal or written, or evidenced by a written memorandum. Clients who are distressed or anxious may not understand clearly all the implications of what they are told at an initial session, and they might not be in the best emotional position to discuss and negotiate terms, or even to remember clearly what was agreed. It is therefore helpful to consider carefully the ethical and practical issues around how (and when) to agree the terms of the therapeutic contract with clients, and if necessary, to revisit and discuss the contract from time to time as therapy progresses.

A requirement for a legally effective contract is that both parties share an understanding of what has been agreed, and they should each therefore have a similar memory of the details of that agreement. Recording a therapeutic contract in writing (or in some other appropriate way) provides a useful *aide-mémoire* for client and therapist and also provides lasting legally acceptable evidence as to what was agreed, should they ever need to refer to it at a later time.

In some circumstances oral contracts might not present any difficulties. However, if the contract is not written down, the lack of any evidence of what has been agreed might become problematic, e.g. if a client considers that they have been misled or harmed in any way. If there is no written record of an agreement, in the event of any dispute there is often no way of satisfactorily establishing what occurred. It would be just one person's word against another. For example, if the disagreement escalated into a legal dispute over confidentiality, the law operates in ways that will generally favour a client claiming a right to confidentiality (see Bond and Mitchels 2008: 127–31). The legal presumption in favour of regarding therapy as confidential is so strong that in the absence of any evidence to the contrary, a court may imply a term of confidentiality and then hold a therapist liable for a breach of the terms created and implied by the court within any legally enforceable contract. Similarly, claims for breach of confidence in common law and under data protection will start with an assumption of a commitment to confidentiality unless the therapist can establish a legal exception based on the client's consent, a statutory duty or the balance of public interest. This means that therapists are legally wise to ensure that clients are informed in advance of any exceptions to confidentiality and that any issues that appear to be significant to either the client, therapist or agency are adequately recorded in ways that could be produced as evidence.

In Scotland the statutory provisions relating to which type of contracts require to be evidenced by writing differ from the provisions in England. Section 1 of the Requirements of Writing (Scotland) Act 1995 lists some of the situations in which writing is required to make a contract legally enforceable. Examples of such situations include contracts which vary rights in land. There is no requirement for a contract for the provision of therapy to be written down. However, as with the position in England, therapists should always ensure that there is adequate written evidence of any contract they enter into, in order to protect themselves in the event of a future dispute.

E-commerce and digital signatures

In modern times, the use of the internet for commerce is developing. Electronic communication via emails and documents sent as attachments, and digital signatures have resulted in specific legislation (in the UK, the Electronic Communications Act 2000, Electronic Commerce (EC Directive) Regulations 2002 and Electronic Signatures Regulations 2002). The general rule is that computer-generated communications, which provide a visible representation or record (which could if necessary be printed out as hard copies), are generally deemed to be 'in writing' as defined by Schedule 1 to the Interpretation Act 1978. If stored on the computer, documents must be retrievable in visible form. There is an unresolved issue about text and pager messages, which can be seen but not printed out as hard copies.

4.1.4 Exclusion clauses

The parties to a contract can exclude specific duties or liabilities, provided that they are reasonable and in 'plain, intelligible language', see Regulation 7(1) of the Unfair Terms in Consumer Contract Regulations 1999 (UTCCR 1999). However, some exclusion clauses are deemed in law to be unfair and so disallowed (see the Unfair Contract Terms Act 1977 (UCTA 1977) and UTCCR 1999).

An exemption clause must clearly cover specific eventualities if it is to be effective, and the burden of proving it falls on the person who seeks to rely on the exclusion. Under the provisions of UCTA 1977, we, as therapists, cannot fully exclude our liability for negligence from therapeutic contracts, nor can we exclude aspects of occupier's liability. Under section 2 of UCTA 1977, negligence is defined as the breach:

(a) of any obligation, arising from the express or implied terms of a contract, to take reasonable care or exercise reasonable skill in the performance of the contract

(b) of any common law duty to take reasonable care or exercise reasonable skill (but not any stricter duty)

(C) of the common duty imposed under the Occupier's Liability Act 1957 or the Occupier's Liability (Northern Ireland) Act 1957

Under UCTA 1977, s. 2(1), any exclusion term or notice in a contract will automatically be ineffective if the negligence results in death or personal injury. If the negligence results in other loss or damage, then the exclusion will be ineffective unless it is deemed in law to be reasonable. Under UTCCR 1999, this is slightly watered down in that a test of fairness is now applied, but it is hard to imagine any circumstances in a therapeutic contract in which such a clause would ever be deemed by the courts to be fair. As this area of law is complex, should any therapist wish to try to exclude their liability for negligence, or should any claimant allege negligence against a therapist, it is advisable to get legal advice on the specific circumstances of the case.

4.2 Therapeutic contracts: creating legally binding agreements with clients

4.2.1 Why do we need a therapeutic contract?

The reasons for entering into a therapeutic contract are ethical, legal and practical. Professional ethics support client autonomy and expect that therapists are trustworthy and practise self-respect. If, therefore, therapists fully communicate and clients fully understand in advance what to expect from therapy, and the terms on which it is offered, and therapists, in contracting, also pay attention to their own needs in addition to those of the client, those ethical principles are likely to be addressed. Clients may then feel more confident and safer to face the challenges of receiving therapy, and they may be more likely to feel satisfied with the therapeutic service provided. Clarity in negotiating the therapeutic contract should therefore help to prevent client dissatisfaction reaching the level that prompts litigation or formal complaints.

It is advisable to provide clients with an opportunity to raise any concerns about aspects of therapy in discussion with the therapist before therapy starts. In that way, potential problems can be discussed and a fully negotiated, mutually acceptable agreement can be reached.

The exploration of contract law in 4.1.2 shows that a prerequisite for a legally effective contract is that both parties share an understanding of what has been agreed, and they should each therefore have a similar memory of the details of that agreement. For the reasons set out in 4.1.3, therapists would be well advised to ensure that any issues that appear to be significant to the client, therapist or agency are adequately recorded as part of the therapeutic contract in ways that could be produced as evidence. See the guidance in BACP Information Sheet P11, *Making the Contract for Counselling and Psychotherapy* (Dale 2008a).

4.2.2 What terms should go into a therapeutic contract?

As discussed in 4.1.2, in order to create an effective and mutually acceptable contract, both parties must first reach a mutual understanding of the scope and terms of their relationship.

Therapists need to consider ethical and professional issues, legal requirements, and any relevant agency policies and procedures. For helpful information from the BACP website, see Information Sheets P11, *Making the Contract for Counselling and Psychotherapy* (Dale 2008a), P2 *Charging for Therapy in Private Practice: Pitfalls and Issues* (Dale 2008b), and the *Ethical Framework* (BACP 2010). In Chapter 12 of *Confidentiality and Record Keeping in Counselling and Psychotherapy* (Bond and Mitchels 2008) we explored some of these issues, using examples of existing contracts in use by colleagues. However, we would encourage therapists to develop their own contracts, compliant with current law and the public interest, and meeting the needs of the therapist, agency and client.

Therapists may sometimes find themselves in a dilemma in which they wish, or are requested by a client, to agree to terms in a therapeutic contract which may run counter to their terms of employment or their agency policy. This may be particularly relevant, for example, regarding issues of confidentiality, making, storing and retaining client records, or when making referrals. They should bear in mind that the courts may enforce explicit contractual agreements, with the possible two exceptions of agreements which conflict with statutory law or would be contrary to the public interest, e.g. by preventing the investigation or detection of serious crime. Agency policy should therefore be compatible with the law and public interest, and in order to avoid conflict, clients should be offered terms in compliance with relevant agency policy. Therapists who disagree with any aspect of their agency policy may need to consider their position carefully and then address and resolve outstanding issues with the agency. High compatibility with law and agency policy creates the best chance of providing a professional service that clients can trust and protection for therapists and others from legal liabilities. Incompatibilities may create tensions within any service, which may lead to successful claims against that service or create conflicts of responsibility and liability for the staff concerned or for their clients.

Clients may complain that the fees for therapy are too high, or that the fee structure for therapy was unclear to the client when therapy commenced. Therapists may complain that clients have not paid the fees due, are late in payment, or refuse to pay for missed sessions. These frustrations might be avoided if fees, payments, cancellation policy, and action following non-payment of fees are discussed and agreed with the client before the work begins. In order to calculate the likely total of fees payable, a client may need to know the hourly rate, session duration, session frequency, and the potential length of therapy.

Discussion of the terms on which therapy is offered does not have to be protracted, difficult or legalistic. Sometimes the creation of the therapeutic contract can be a helpful part of the therapeutic process, providing an opportunity to build trust, explore relevant issues, create mutual understanding and to develop a therapeutic alliance. If a client is anxious and/or their mental state is not conducive to concentration on details or remembering terms, an initial discussion may be followed by revisiting the contract again as appropriate as therapy progresses. It is helpful to provide advance information about therapy, and the terms on which it is offered. This can be in various forms, for example leaflets, posters, entries in directories or web pages, and advertisements. Advance information may shorten and facilitate the initial discussion about the terms of the therapeutic contract. If that discussion is then supported by a written or other tangible record of the agreement, clients are helped to assimilate information and to refer to and recall what was agreed. If clients are also made aware that they (or the therapist) can raise issues about their contract again during the course of therapy if they wish to do so, then client autonomy is respected and the contract may be renegotiated at a later date.

Checklist: Elements to consider for inclusion in the therapeutic contract

- Names, addresses
- Contact details (and any limitations)
- Fee structure and policy (hourly rate, charges for missed sessions, fee for time spent in phone calls, writing reports, action on non-payment, etc.)

- Frequency and duration of sessions (will dates and times be fixed and regular or will each appointment be negotiated?)
- Likely duration of therapy (e.g. is it time-limited or open-ended, and if open-ended, are estimated duration and/or regular reviews necessary for funding or other purposes?)
- Policy for non-attendance (e.g. will therapy be withdrawn for non-attendance without reasonable excuse or explanation?)
- Holidays
- Cancellation of sessions by therapist or the client
- Terminating therapy (deciding when and how to end therapy)
- Contact between sessions (when and where can the client call the therapist?)
- Confidentiality issues (e.g. the legal limits of confidentiality. Does the client consent to share information? In what circumstances? Referral procedures and client instructions and consents)
- Any information and consents relevant for possible referrals
- Record keeping (e.g. how long will records be kept?)
- Client rights of access to records
- Use of records for supervision, research, audit, etc.
- Relevant data protection issues and any explicit consents required for sensitive personal data
- Tape and other recordings of sessions (ownership, access, potential uses and retention)
- Counsellor's professional memberships, code of ethics, insurance and information about complaints procedures.

Case history and referral information may be sought and specific aspects can be reflected in the contract if this is appropriate: or for the safety of the client or others.

- relevant case history
- general practitioner details
- other professionals' reports
- other professionals, agencies, family or friends to be contacted with the client's consent if therapeutically necessary or appropriate to support the client or for the safety of the client or others.

4.3 Complex interlinking professional relationships

Examples of possible multiple interlinking relationships:

- trainee / placement / training institution / supervision
- therapist / employer, agency or organisation / supervisor
- therapist / academic institution and external examiners / clients / supervision.

Where a therapist is in training, they may undertake to have personal therapy, and an essential condition of most training courses is that the trainees undertake to have professional supervision for their work. Trainees may find themselves with a training contract in which supervision is a condition, and the supervisor is

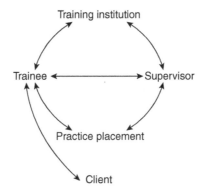

Figure 4.1   Trainees' potential contractual relationships

required to make periodical reports to the training establishment with the consent of the trainee. There may also be a duty imposed on the supervisor (to which the trainee agrees) to inform both the trainee and the training establishment if the trainee is for any reason unfit to practise or to continue training, or where the trainee's practice becomes potentially harmful to clients.

The same applies to trainees, training institutions and training placements. Sometimes, in a placement, supervision is linked in with management responsibilities within the placement. There may be group or peer supervision arrangements, perhaps in addition to individual supervision for the trainee, which may be provided by the placement internally or externally.

These monitoring arrangements during training are set up for the protection of clients and the trainee therapist, and are necessary as part of the ethical and professional responsibilities of training. It is helpful to ensure that each person involved in the arrangements understands the role of the others involved, and is willing to comply with the proposed arrangements. The contract between the supervisor and the trainee may contain conditions requested by the training institution. Often, institutions will provide draft contract terms for the trainees and their supervisors.

It may be, for the reasons explored in the preceding paragraphs, that these complex relationships could be addressed in one contract between all the parties involved, but usually the duties and responsibilities are dealt with by separate (but interlinked or cross-referenced) contracts. For example between:

- Trainee, training institution and placement agency. This is best dealt with by a three-way contract, available to all the parties, which records that the training institution has a duty to assess trainees for their readiness to begin client work and to assess the trainee's progress in training, and that the placement agency's aims, procedures and resources are compatible with the trainee's therapeutic approach and that the placement is appropriate for the course. Note: BACP Information Sheet T3, *Guidance for Trainee Placements* (Coates 2004), sets out recommendations for issues to be included in explicit written agreements between trainees, placement agency and training course providers.

- Trainee and supervisor, possibly incorporating terms requested by the training institution.
- Therapist and client, possibly noting the trainee status of the therapist and incorporating specific conditions, e.g. in dealing with tape-recorded sessions, client notes etc., in assessment and training.

4.4 Contract issues when working with couples and families

Many therapists have situations where they are working 'one to one' with a client, who may then request that their spouse, partner or a family member attends a session with them. The therapist may feel that the presence of the other person(s) will assist the therapeutic work, e.g. in relationship issues, and agree to have sessions with those people present. Later, the therapy may revert back to one-to-one sessions with the original client again.

In this situation, it helps to give some thought to the issues (e.g. 'Who is my client?' and 'What is my responsibility to each person present?'), before providing the joint sessions. If a clear agreement is reached with the client and all other parties in the sessions, particularly about boundaries and confidentiality, this will help should any disputes between the clients arise in the future, for example after the family or couple breaks up. If the case comes to court, everyone has a clear understanding of their rights in the event of the therapist being asked to give evidence or produce notes of the sessions.

The therapist should have formed a therapeutic contract with the original client, including the issue of confidentiality. When any other person comes to join in with one or more sessions, e.g. for couple or family work, there should be a further discussion about the (revised) terms of the therapy, including confidentiality at that stage, because now there may be two (or more) 'clients' for that session. For example, if a man comes to therapy which includes anger management, he may ask for his wife to join in some of his therapy sessions to discuss relationships at home and perhaps to develop strategies to manage stressors within the family. The original therapeutic contract was with the client alone, and so now the therapist, client and his wife need to form a separate contractual agreement for their joint sessions. They may both agree, for example, that they will not share information from the session with any other family members without the consent of the other. Any differences or tensions between the couple over notes, sharing information, payment, etc., may need to be clarified and resolved. If the therapy then subsequently reverts back to the original client, then the terms of the 'original' one-to-one therapeutic contract should be briefly revisited and may need clarification for those subsequent sessions.

In Chapter 3 we looked at the law of tort. Under that law, there is also a duty of care to all the parties in couple or family therapy, which includes an implied duty of confidentiality. So, now bearing in mind the law of contract and tort together, we have an implied duty of confidentiality and a need for a clear therapeutic contract with the therapist for those joint sessions which includes discussion about notes, information sharing, etc. It does not matter whether we might call the joint sessions 'couple counselling' or 'family work', or even if we had simply thought of it as 'inviting a husband to attend a client session with his wife'.

The need for clarity about rights and responsibilities in a therapeutic contract is particularly evident in situations where the parties may develop a dispute, leading to court action. An example might be that a therapist is working with a husband who has a gambling problem. His wife had been invited to participate in one therapy session, in which he admitted that he had gambled several times in the past and lied about it to her. Some time later, she leaves him and there is a contested divorce. In the court proceedings, he denies his gambling, and she asks the therapist to provide evidence of his admissions. The husband does not want the therapist to disclose that information. If the therapist had made a clear contract with both husband and wife to keep their joint session confidential, she is bound by her contract to keep that confidence for both parties, unless the court orders her to disclose the information. Even if the therapist has no clear contract with the husband and the wife, she still has a duty of care to both parties, and it is our view that she would be justified in waiting for an order of the court before she discloses the requested information. On the other hand, it might be justifiable to breach a contractual term in order to fulfil a duty of care to the partner if the other person is threatening imminent and significant physical harm or a serious criminal offence against them.

4.5 Remedies for breach of contract

4.5.1 Can I change my mind and get out of a contract?

If both parties agree to end a contract by mutual agreement, then there is no problem. The difficulties arise where one party wants to terminate a contract and the other wants to hold them to it, or penalise them for breaking it. The law allows a party to get out of a contract for specific reasons:

- misrepresentation
- mistake
- duress and undue influence
- illegality and public policy.

Misrepresentation

Misrepresentation is where a party makes a positive statement of fact which is adopted by the other party but is untrue (e.g. a client enters into a therapeutic contract because the therapist specifically claims to be fully qualified and accredited by the BACP when the truth is that they are still in training).

In contract law, to be misrepresentation, it does not matter whether the statement was made deliberately or carelessly, innocently or fraudulently. Misrepresentation can be by writing, or by pictures or drawings, and even silent actions can take on significance in certain contexts. An example might be a client who goes to a therapist because his name is on a website exclusively for counsellors specialising in a specific modality, and the therapist, by being included on that site is holding himself out to be such a specialist when in fact he is not. The penalty for misrepresentation depends on the circumstances and options may include avoidance or rescission of the contract, or damages (see 4.5.2 below). Under s. 2(1) of the Misrepresentation Act 1967, damages can be awarded for negligent misrepresentation.

How much detail do we have to disclose to be considered truthful? The courts are reasonable on this. For example, in answer to a question about health when asked to mention any visits to the doctor in the past, a person would not be expected to list every visit since birth. A truthful answer for practical purposes might be to list those made recently and those that were important, see *Joel* v *Law Union & Crown Insurance* [1908] 2 KB 863 CA.

If a vendor sells an item knowing what it really is, but stating that it is something different, that is a deliberate (and fraudulent) misrepresentation. So therapists must be open and honest about their qualifications and experience, and not claim qualifications they do not have.

Trading (advertising and selling) items with false descriptions can potentially result not only in civil remedies but in criminal prosecution (see the Consumer Protection from Unfair Trading Regulations 2008, which replaced most of the old Trade Descriptions Act 1968). The new regulations apply to unfair commercial practice and apply to promotion, sale or supply of a product to consumers. 'Business' includes a profession, and 'product' includes any services, and so we would suggest that it therefore includes therapy. The regulations prohibit any misleading actions or omissions which are likely to cause the average consumer to make a different transactional decision, e.g. to make a purchase, or have work done, or accept a service that he might not otherwise have made. Misleading actions and omissions include giving false descriptions of the nature, attributes and rights of the trader, which include his identity, qualifications, status, approval, affiliations or connections (see regulation 5(6)). A therapist who falsely claims BACP accreditation could, we suggest, fall within these regulations.

We are not yet aware of case law on the new regulations, but guidance is available from each local Trading Standards Service, for which online guidance can be found here: www.tradingstandards.gov.uk/advice/consumer-advice.cfm. Failure to comply with these regulations is a criminal offence, which could lead to a fine and/or imprisonment. Civil remedies and enforcement are also available.

Misrepresentation by a person wanting insurance might include the non-disclosure of material facts at the time of the contract or renewal. (A material fact might be, for example, that a therapist is subject to ongoing disciplinary proceedings which, if known, might influence the insurance cover offered). If the insurance company wanted to use the non-disclosure as a reason to rescind the contract, they would have to prove it. A defence would be that the insurers already know of the fact, or that it was waived by the insurer. For further discussion and examples of insurance matters, see Chapter 6. If non-disclosure is fraudulent, then that may constitute the tort of deceit and damages might be awarded (see the comments of Lord Rix in the case of *HIH* v *Chase Manhattan* [2001] EWCA Civ 1250, 2 Lloyds Rep 483 at page 163, and [2003] UKHL 6 [2003] Lloyds Rep IR 230, and Table 4.1 at 4.5.2 below).

Mistake

In legal terms, a mistake is a false belief or assumption. Mistakes can be made by one or both parties. They might both be mistaken in the same way, e.g. both commonly believing something when it is not true. One of them may be mistaken, and then they are at cross purposes. Mistakes can be fundamental, the subject matter being 'essentially and radically different' from what the parties believe it to be. Mistakes may, for example, involve the nature, quality or quantity of the goods or services.

There are several types of mistake, and they are seen differently in law:

- Both parties share the same mistaken belief (common mistake)
- One party has a mistaken belief and the other is unaware of it
- One party has a mistaken belief and the other *is* aware of the mistake but does not correct it
- A record of an agreement is incorrect
- A party signs an essential document in the erroneous belief that it is something else.

The way that the law responds to mistakes depends on whether the actions are perceived by the court as deliberate misrepresentation, fraud or deceit. From the examples above, it will be clear that some situations involve mistakes that are not intentional or fraudulent. Deliberate fraud may lead not only to civil action but result in criminal prosecution.

A person has no legal right to change their mind and get out of a contract just because they have made a mistake. For example, a person who chooses and buys a red sweater, thinking that it will match other clothes and then finds on getting home that it does not, has no automatic legal right to bring it back for exchange. Sellers that allow customers to return or exchange goods unconditionally, do so for the goodwill, not because they have to (see Furmston 2007: 878–945).

In the context of providing therapy, it is essential to ensure that clients understand clearly the nature and terms of the service being offered. Clients may mistakenly expect a certain type of treatment and feel aggrieved when the therapy or service they receive is not what they had expected.

Duress and undue influence

When a person enters a contract but not of their own free and independent will, in some circumstances, the law allows them to get out of it. In legal terminology, as Malcolm Clark succinctly puts it, 'Duress is the pressure of the big stick or the bottom line. Undue influence is the pressure of personality.' There is also the further category of 'actual undue influence', in which there is a threat to the physical as well as emotional well-being of the person threatened (Clark 2007: 945–6).

It is feasible that a child or young person or vulnerable adult might be persuaded or induced in some way by others to see a therapist, but it is unlikely that a therapist, once made aware of this situation, would agree to continue to provide therapy on that basis. To do so would raise serious ethical issues, for example about client autonomy, beneficience, non-maleficience and justice, and may constitute grounds for complaint (BACP 2009). Vulnerable adults in need of compulsory therapy may legally be admitted for treatment subject to compliance with the Mental Health Act 2007, Mental Health (Care and Treatment) (Scotland) Act 2003 and/or the Mental Capacity Act 2005, which are there for their protection, and children in need of compulsory medical or psychological treatment are subject to the child protection legislation and to the jurisdiction of the High Court (see 4.7).

Illegality and public policy

Parties who enter into a contract to do something illegal (e.g. an agreement to sell illegal drugs or offering confidentiality to an active terrorist about an intended terrorist attack) or contrary to public policy may be committing a serious criminal offence as well as giving grounds for civil action. Any contract based on an act that is expressly prohibited as illegal is void. The status of contracts contrary to public policy is less clear, because public policy changes from time to time. Most actions contrary to public policy are also illegal. If caught up in a questionable situation, seek legal advice.

4.5.2 Ending contracts

Contracts may end because both parties have fulfilled their obligations, for example, they have reached the agreed ending of therapy. However, one party to a contract may, for some reason, want to end a contract before the conditions are all fulfilled, and in this situation the law may govern why, how and when the contract is ended.

The law allows the ending of a contract:

- when both parties agree
- when one of the parties has a right to end it (e.g. for misrepresentation)
- when the contract is 'frustrated', i.e. it cannot be fulfilled (e.g. a therapy contract with a soldier who is unexpectedly posted overseas)
- where a party has broken (in legal terms, 'breached') the terms of the contract.

There are also other more complex legal situations, but we need not go into them here. When a contract ends before it is fulfilled, the parties (and if there are disputes, the courts) have to decide how to settle the situation fairly. Often, commercial contracts have clauses which make provision for premature endings. There is no reason why therapeutic contracts should not also look at what the therapist and client would like to happen if their contract ended early.

A common situation is where one of the parties breaches the terms of the contract. Examples from therapy might be a client's failure to pay, a therapist (or client) not turning up for sessions, or a breach of confidentiality by the therapist without the client's consent.

Paragraph 4.5.3 below and Table 4.1 provide a brief outline of some of the remedies and penalties for breach of contract.

TABLE 4.1   Remedies awarded in contract law

Event	Penalty
Misrepresentation	
Fraudulent	Rescission and/or damages under s. 2, Misrepresentation Act 1967
Negligent	Rescission and/or damages under s. 2 Misrepresentation Act 1967
Non-disclosure	
Fraudulent	Rescission and/or damages
Misstatement	
Negligent misstatement	Damages for all types of loss which are a reasonable consequence of the misstatement
Misstatement	Damages for foreseeable loss
Mistake	Possibly contract void
	Damages
Failure to fulfil the contract	Specific performance
	Literal enforcement (orders to do whatever was promised)
	Damages

Note: Damages take many forms. See 4.5.3 for definitions, authorities and discussion of assessment of damages.

4.5.3 Breach of contract – penalties and remedies

Penalties and remedies for breach of contract:

- **Rescission**, i.e. giving and taking back on both sides to restore the situation before the contract took place. Examples include exchange, return of goods and refund, etc.
- **Voiding the contract**, i.e. cancelling the whole contract.
- **Damages**, i.e. payment of money as compensation for a loss.

Rescission and voiding contracts

Both these remedies aim to restore the situation for the parties as it was before the contract was made. Rescission is an ending to the contract, and restoration may be, for example, by returning goods and refunding any payments made. Voiding a contract is treating it as if it had never existed, and again, restoration may also take place.

These remedies are useful in commercial contracts but, in the context of therapy, in a situation where therapy has already started it might not be possible to restore the situation as it was before the contract. The therapy, however brief, may already have effected changes for both client and therapist. Rescission and avoidance in this situation may be of little practical use.

Damages

'Damages' is the legal term for a financial award to compensate for some sort of loss and may be awarded for negligence or breach of contract. In order to succeed in a claim for damages for breach of contract, the claimant needs to prove on a balance of probabilities:

* a loss
* a breach of the contract leading to the loss alleged.

The other party may state by way of defence (answer) to a claim for damages that the loss was not entirely attributable to the failure of the contract, or in some other way the loss was not entirely their fault and/or that the claimant might have suffered a smaller loss if they had done (or not done) something to mitigate it. The court will then consider the facts of each case to assess the amount of damages to be awarded.

The law concerning damages for breach of contract has many complicated rules and the amount of any damages awarded must depend largely upon the particular circumstances of each case.

The rules and exceptions about assessment of damages are very complicated and it is advisable to seek legal and/or financial advice in an action about breach of contract because most cases are settled out of court and parties need to ensure that they settle for a fair sum. See Table 4.1 for an overview of the main remedies awarded in different contract situations.

4.5.4 Interest for late payment of debts – how to encourage prompt payment!

Therapists may be very pleased to know that in situations where they have been commissioned to undertake work for which they have not been paid on time, they can charge interest. The Late Payment of Commercial Debts (Interest) Act 1998, as amended by subsequent legislation, allows interest to be charged for the late payment of contracts for goods or services where both parties are acting in the course of a business. Interest (currently set by the rules at the generous rate of 8 per cent over the base rate) is payable from either an agreed date in the contract or within 30 days after delivery or invoice, whichever is the later.

Therapists and other professionals have told us that they use this legislation to successfully avoid problems and long delays in payment, by simply adding a suitable clause at the end of each invoice. For example: Payment for this invoice should be remitted within 30 working days, after which interest will be charged in accordance with the Late Payment of Commercial Debts [Interest] Act 1998.

4.6 Capacity and contract-making: vulnerable adults

A client's ability to give legally valid consent to any medical, psychiatric or therapeutic assessment or treatment, or to enter into either a valid therapeutic contract or a legally binding contact for services, will depend upon their mental capacity to make an informed decision.

Mental capacity is a legal concept, according to which a person's ability to make rational, informed decisions is assessed, and for adults, this is now governed by the Mental Capacity Act 2005, the Mental Health Act 2007 and The Mental Capacity Act 2005 (Appropriate Body) (England) Regulations 2006. Relevant publications and websites are listed at the end of this book. For the relevant provisions as they apply to Scotland, see the Adults with Incapacity (Scotland) Act 2000 and the Mental Health (Care and Treatment) (Scotland) Act 2003.

There is no single test for mental capacity to consent. Assessment of mental capacity is not on a theoretical ability to make decisions generally, but is situation-specific and depends upon the ability of the person to:

- take in and understand information, including the risks and benefits of the decision to be made, and
- retain the information long enough to weigh up the factors to make the decision, and
- communicate their wishes.

Part 1 of the Mental Capacity Act 2005 (MCA), which came into force on 1 October 2007, defines 'persons who lack capacity' and sets out relevant principles to be applied, including a checklist to be used to ascertain their best interests. In particular, it requires that a person is not to be treated as lacking capacity simply because they may be making an unwise decision.

A person may be mentally incapacitated on a temporary basis (i.e. following an accident or illness), or on a longer-term or permanent basis (i.e. those who suffer from severe long-term mental illness or other impairment of mental functioning) and in their case capacity to make medical decisions is likely to be assessed by a medical doctor or psychiatrist. The assessment of a person's mental capacity for other tasks may be made by others. For example, the decision on their capacity to make a will may be made by a lawyer, or the decision on whether they can engage in therapy may be made by the therapist. If there is any doubt, advice from an appropriate registered medical practitioner, psychiatrist or psychologist should be sought. If there is a dispute about a person's mental capacity to make an important medical decision, the matter should be referred to the High Court or Court of

Session, which will then assist and, if necessary, make a ruling. A person's capacity is relevant in therapy when considering whether someone can give a valid consent to receive therapy or agree to the terms on which therapy is being provided.

4.7 Capacity and contract-making: children and young people under the age of 18

The concept of children and young people under the age of 18 making a therapeutic contract combines two separate areas of law. The first is the law of contract, under which 'minors' are allowed, because of their age, to back out of certain types of contract for goods and services. The other is the separate line of law about the capacity of children of different ages, maturity and understanding to give their consent (or refusal) for medical treatment, therapy and advice, and therefore their ability to enter into a therapeutic contract and request confidentiality.

The law on children's capacity to make decisions and on other people making decisions for children is vitally important for all practitioners who work with children and young people, and so we consider it in some detail. In order to address the question of children making therapeutic contracts, we need to look first at the position of 'minors' in the context of contract law. We will then explore the decision-making capacity of children of different ages. Finally, we will bring these two areas of law together.

4.7.1 Contract law and minors

Children and young people under the age of 18 are collectively referred to in many areas of law (including contract law) as 'minors'. People over the age of 18 are said to have reached the age of 'majority'. Section 1 of the Family Law Reform Act 1969 lowered the former age of majority of 21 to the present age of 18. The Children Act 1989 defines a 'child' as 'a person under the age of 18' (s. 105) and there is a similar provision in the Children (Scotland) Act 1995, s. 15(1).

In the old common law of contract, as amended by the more recent Minors' Contracts Act 1987, subject to some exceptions, minors are not generally held to be legally bound by their contracts, and they are therefore able to go back on them. The old law was originally designed to protect minors, but it also led to cases where unscrupulous minors ran up huge bills and the creditors could not then recover their money. As a result, some people were understandably reluctant to supply minors with goods or services. Since it was also recognised that minors might need to eat, dress, travel, work and live somewhere, exceptions were developed to allow minors to enter into legally enforceable contracts for 'necessary goods and services', as well as beneficial contracts of employment, e.g. apprenticeship. The Sale of Goods Act 1979 in s. 3 makes a minor liable to pay a reasonable price for necessary goods purchased, provided that they are 'goods suitable to the condition of life' of the minor 'at the time of sale or delivery'.

Legal advice is a 'necessary' service' and payments for medical attention were also considered 'necessary' at least until the advent of the NHS. If therapeutic contracts fall within the definition of 'necessary services', then they are legally enforceable. In practice, enforcement of a therapeutic contract against a young person who is unwilling to continue with it raises ethical and therapeutic issues, and since contractual disputes are likely to be over payment or confidentiality, a more positive and ethical approach would be a review and renegotiation of the therapeutic alliance.

Contract law and minors in Scotland

In Scotland, the general rule is that children under the age of 16 cannot enter into contracts. However, it was recognised that under 16s do as a matter of fact regularly enter into contractual relationships, for instance through the purchase of small items such as bus tickets and sweets. For that reason, there is an exception to the general rule allowing those under the age of 16 to enter into a contract which is of a kind commonly entered into by people of that age, and where the terms of the contract are not unreasonable. Whether a therapeutic contract falls within the category of an 'agreement commonly entered into' by persons under the age of 16 is not clear.

The general rule in relation to 16 and 17 year olds in Scotland is that they do have the capacity to contract on their own behalf. However, as with under 16s, there is an exception to the general rule. Where a 16 or 17 year old has entered into a 'prejudicial transaction', then the transaction can be challenged. A transaction will be deemed to be prejudicial where the following two criteria are met:

1. An adult exercising reasonable prudence would not have entered into the transaction.
2. The transaction has caused or is likely to cause substantial prejudice to young person.

An application to set aside a prejudicial transaction can be made in the Court of Session or in the Sheriff Court.

4.7.2 Children: their capacity to make decisions and therapeutic contracts

Whether children can enter into a therapeutic contract will depend upon whether they have the legal capacity to make their own decisions.

Children aged 16–18

Under s. 8(1) of the Family Law Reform Act 1969 and s. 1 of the Age of Legal Capacity (Scotland) Act 1991, a child of age 16 or over may make his or her own medical decisions and therefore they may also make therapeutic contracts.

Children under age 16 – 'Gillick competence'

Children who are under the age of 16 may be competent to make their own decisions. This principle of law was settled by the House of Lords in the leading case of *Gillick* v *West Norfolk and Wisbech Area Health Authority and Another* [1986]

1 AC 1212; [1985] 3 All ER 402 (HL) [1986] 1 FLR 224. See also s. 2(1) and (4) of the Age of Legal Capacity (Scotland) Act 1991.

The rationale of the *Gillick* case was that a child's ability to make an informed decision depends upon a number of factors, including the:

- nature and seriousness of the decision to be made
- child's age
- child's maturity
- child's contextual understanding of the circumstances
- information given to the child to enable them to understand the potential benefits and risks of what is proposed and the consequences of consent or refusal.

It will be evident that the capacity of a child to make a decision is situation-specific, and that the child must have an informed understanding of the issues, including the risks and benefits involved and the consequences of refusal, before they can be considered to be '*Gillick* competent'.

The ability to help a child make a decision will depend on the provision of age-appropriate information and explanations or answers to their questions. The more serious the decision, the greater is the need for the child to possess sufficient maturity and understanding to evaluate their situation in its wider context. For this reason, the courts have steadfastly refused to set specific age limits for *Gillick* competence.

Each case involving a child client must be decided on its own merits. If the child is under 16, it is the task of the therapist, with other professional help if necessary, to talk through the situation with the child client. Together, they will need to explore and discuss the child's circumstances and the options available, considering the possible outcome of each option open to the child, and then decide whether the child has the capacity to make the necessary decisions, including whether to enter into a therapeutic contract. The same process is necessary in the context of a therapeutic relationship when helping a child to assess whether they will require the therapist to keep confidentiality or to make a referral.

Consent for a therapeutic contract can be given for a young child under the age of 16 who is not '*Gillick* competent' by:

- a person with parental responsibility for the child
- an order of the High Court or Court of Session.

If therapeutic treatment is considered necessary and the child or those with parental responsibility refuse, or if there is any issue about the competence of a child to make an informed decision, the matter can, if necessary, be referred to those with parental responsibility for the child and/or for expert opinion and/or to the High Court. The High Court has the power to make an order in the best interests of the child and resolve disputes with a 'Specific issue' order made under s. 8 of the Children Act 1989 or s. 11(2)(e) of the Children (Scotland) Act 1995. Bond and Mitchels (2008: Chapter 11) discuss the right of children and young people to refuse medical examination or treatment in detail.

Once a young person reaches 18 years of age even the High Court cannot over-rule their wishes about medical examination, treatment or therapy unless for any reason they lack the mental capacity to make their own decision.

Emergency medical or psychiatric treatment

If medically necessary and there is a grave risk to the child if emergency treatment is not given, medical practitioners may rely on their own clinical judgement if those in a position to give consent are unavailable.

4.7.3 Parental responsibility

People may assume that all parents have the power to make decisions for their children. This is emphatically (and perhaps surprisingly) not so. The ability of a parent, or anyone else, to make a decision for their child depends on whether they have 'parental responsibility', which is the legal basis for making decisions about a child, including consent for therapy. It was created by the Children Act 1989, and defined in s. 3(1) as 'all the rights, duties, powers, responsibilities and authority which by law the parent of a child has in relation to a child and his property'. There may be new legislation which will further define the concept of parental responsibil-ity, so watch for changes in the law. See also the Children (Scotland) Act 1995, s. 1.

More than one person can have parental responsibility for a child at the same time. Parental responsibility cannot be transferred or surrendered, but elements may be delegated (see the Children Act 1989, s. 2(9) and Children (Scotland) Act 1995, s. 3(5)).

Who has parental responsibility?

Bond and Mitchels (2008: Chapter 11) discuss the complex law of parental respon-sibility in detail. Here is a brief summary:

Mothers and married fathers. Every mother (whether she is married or not) has parental responsibility for each child born to her, and every father who is married to the child's mother at the time of or subsequent to the conception of their child automatically has parental responsibility for their child, which may be shared with others, but will cease only on death or adoption.

Unmarried fathers. Unmarried fathers may acquire parental responsibility for their biological child in one of several ways, the first three of which can only be removed by order of the court:

- From 1 December 2003, in England an unmarried father automatically acquires parental responsibility for his child if, with his consent, he is named as the child's father on the registration of the child's birth. This law does not operate retrospectively. (For similar provisions in Scotland, see the Family Law (Scotland) Act 2006, s. 23.)

- By formal 'Parental Responsibility Agreement' signed by the mother and father, witnessed by an officer at court, then registered. Copies may be obtained for a fee, in a similar way to obtaining a birth certificate – see Parental Responsibility Agreement Regulations 1991 and the Children (Scotland) Act 1995, s. 4.
- The court can make an order under s. 4(1)(a) of the Children Act 1989, awarding parental responsibility to him, consistent with the interests of the child.

Parental responsibility (PR) can also be acquired by a child's biological father where:

- a residence order is made under s. 8 of the Children Act 1989, directing the child to live with the father, and PR is awarded along with it
- appointment as child's guardian made under s. 5 of the Children Act 1989
- marriage to the child's mother
- certain placement or adoption orders under the Adoption and Children Act 2002.

Acquisition of parental responsibility by others including civil partners. Parental responsibility may be acquired by others including civil partners, in a variety of ways. It may also be shared with those who already have it in relation to the child. In some cases, the exercise of parental responsibility may be limited by the court. For details, see Bond and Mitchels (2008: chapter 11).

What if there is no one with parental responsibility for a child?

Some children, for example the child of a single mother (biological father unknown), who dies without appointing a guardian, may have nobody with legal parental responsibility for them. Relatives or others wishing to care for the child will then have to apply for parental responsibility under one of the applications listed above or, failing that, the local authority has a responsibility to assume the care of the child and can seek an appropriate order.

There is an additional provision in s. 3(5) of the Children Act 1989 that those without parental responsibility may 'do what is reasonable in all the circumstances to safeguard and promote the welfare' of a child in their care. This provision is useful in day-to-day situations, e.g. allowing a babysitter, neighbour or relative, who is temporarily looking after a child, to take that child for medical help in an emergency (see also s. 5 of the Children (Scotland) Act 1995). This provision is unlikely to apply to counselling, unless in an emergency.

5 Therapists and Criminal Activity

What kind of criminal activity might I come across in my work?

I have heard about 'tipping off', but what is it?

If a client tells me about something criminal that they have done, or are about to do, must I report it?

What if I find out that my colleague has done something criminal?

I was caught travelling without a rail ticket last week – is that going to bring the profession into disrepute?

My colleague, a fellow therapist, was found guilty last year of downloading porn on his home computer. What are the professional consequences likely to be for him? Will he have to leave the profession?

What if my clients bring drugs into the therapy room and I do not know? How would it be different if I did know?

My 14 year-old client told me that her (much older) boyfriend got her drunk at a party and then had sex with her. What should I do?

What exactly is harassment? If a former client harasses me, what can I do about it?

At the head of this chapter are some of the questions that we are asked by the hundreds of therapists with whom we are in contact. At any time in the course of their work, therapists might come across every type of human behaviour. Clients can be unimaginably courageous, virtuous or criminal. If we are lucky, we are not faced with too many litigious issues, but the situations that seem to trouble us most are usually those that pose moral dilemmas and those that involve some sort of criminal activity. A particularly difficult situation to resolve is the suspected criminal activity of a client or colleague. This chapter looks at some of the issues that could affect therapists in the context of their work.

5.1 What kind of criminal activity might I come across in my work?

Certain areas of therapy will pose their own specific risks. For example, working in a drug rehabilitation unit or with active drug users may lead to the therapist hearing from the client about their ongoing illegal use of drugs and/or stealing to get money for drugs or the possibility of a client bringing illegal drugs into the therapy room or on to the premises.

Therapists working with children and young people may hear about all manner of forms of abuse in which their client is a victim (and sometimes a perpetrator), such as neglect and physical, emotional or sexual abuse. Therapists working with vulnerable adults may also hear about similar forms of abuse. Any of these may, according to its nature and severity, constitute an illegal act or a serious crime.

Therapists working with clients with problems of personality or anger management may threaten violence to others, while others may threaten self-harm. Although self-harm and suicide are not in themselves illegal, they may become illegal where the planned actions involve potential serious harm to others, e.g. by parking on a railway line, starting a fire, deliberately driving into oncoming traffic or jumping off a bridge on to a busy road.

Therapists working in any situation, with any client, may hear about things that the client has done and is perhaps ashamed of, or thinks that they may have got away with. This could potentially include any sort of criminal activity. Offences reported by clients might, for example, include shoplifting, financial fraud, selling illegal drugs, road traffic offences such as drink driving, criminal damage and acts of harassment or even terrorism.

The problem that the therapist is faced with is what (if anything), as a responsible citizen and professional, should we do about it? In 5.2, we discuss some of the questions we are often asked.

5.2 If a client tells me about something criminal that they have done or are about to do, must I report it?

In some cases, under statute law, certain criminal offences *must* be reported. Other offences *may* be reported, and the courts would be sympathetic to the therapist's actions in the event of a court case being brought against them by the client, e.g. for damages for breach of confidentiality, on the basis that the therapist acted in the public interest, which outweighs the interests of an individual client. In other cases, it is possible that the courts may not be so sympathetic to the therapist, and so the therapist must make their own decision about what to do, based on their agency policies and rules, their professional guidance and ethical framework, and their own conscience and professional judgement. They will then have to stand by their decision, and deal with the consequences of any legal action brought against them by their client. These three categories are explored below in 5.2.1, with examples.

5.2.1 Obligations to disclose information about certain criminal offences

1. Criminal offences where the law requires compulsory disclosure
Terrorism and terrorist activities   In the law relating to the prevention and detection of terrorism, it is a legal duty under section 38B of the Terrorism Act 2000 to disclose information about terrorist activities.

Under s. 19 of that Act, it is a separate criminal offence to fail to disclose information acquired in the course of a trade, profession, business or employment about certain actions in support of terrorism, for example fundraising (s. 15), use of money or property (s. 16), funding arrangements (s. 17) and money laundering (s. 18). For further discussion, see Bond and Mitchels (2008: 33–41).

Under s. 39, there is a further offence of 'tipping off', which we discuss in 5.3 below.

Drug trafficking and drug money laundering   Under s. 52 of the Drug Trafficking Act 1994, it is an offence (without reasonable excuse) to fail to disclose information acquired in the course of a trade, profession, business or employment about drug money laundering. Under ss. 53 and 58, it is an offence to 'tip off' a person that a drug money laundering investigation is being made or to prejudice such an investigation.

2. Serious crimes that may be reported with some degree of legal immunity for the reporting therapist (defensible disclosure)

Therapists working within the government agencies and organisations, e.g. the NHS or social services, must comply with statutory duties and agency policies as part of their conditions of employment. Those working in non-governmental agencies must comply with the law and are bound by their contract of employment.

Any therapist acting in good faith may, at their discretion, notify the relevant authorities about serious crime, with a degree of legal protection in the event of a civil case being brought against the therapist in respect of the disclosure. Serious crimes include preventing (or assisting detection of) drug trafficking and money laundering – see the Drug Trafficking Act 1994 and the Proceeds of Crime Act 2002.

Lord Justice Bingham stated the common law position in the case of *W v Egdell and Others* [1990] 2WLR 471, confirming that the public interest in the prevention and detection of serious crime is considered by the courts to be greater than in protecting confidences. Therefore, the courts are unlikely to impose penalties for a breach of confidence which is in the public interest. Such disclosures are described as 'defensible'. It follows that a client cannot effectively insist on confidentiality over a serious crime.

There is no clear definition of a 'serious crime', but the Department of Health offered the following guidance:

> Murder, manslaughter, rape, treason, kidnapping, child abuse or other cases where individuals have suffered serious harm may all warrant breaching confidentiality. Serious harm to the security of the state or to public order and crimes that involve substantial financial gain and loss will generally fall within this category. In contrast, theft, fraud or damage to property where loss or damage is less substantial would generally not warrant breach of confidence. (DH 2003: 35)

An example of a defensible disclosure would include the prevention of serious physical harm likely to be inflicted by a client on another adult, where the information is given in good faith, reasonably well founded, restricted to that which is necessary to prevent the harm, and communicated in confidence to either the authorities or the intended victim.

Guidance relating to child protection envisages disclosure (DfES 2006a, b and c; DH 2000). See Bond and Mitchels (2008: 31–41) for discussion of disclosures. Psychotherapists and counsellors are less likely to acquire the kind of information that is required to be reported under the Drug Trafficking Act 1994, Proceeds of Crime Act 2002 or the Money Laundering Regulations 2007. Although not mentioned in the Department of Health guidance, in serious cases, disclosure of this type of information may be justified on the balance of public interest, but if there is any doubt, seek legal advice. Therapists' professional indemnity insurers often provide free legal advice as part of their cover.

3. Other criminal offences may be reported at the therapist's discretion, but the therapist must deal with any legal consequences of doing so, e.g. claims for breach of confidentiality within the therapeutic contract, etc.

Here, the therapist has to consider the overall requirements of relevant law, professional boundaries and ethics, the therapeutic contract, client needs, and the therapist's own self-respect.

There is a potential dilemma regarding disclosure in any situation where a therapist knows that a client is likely to harm another person. This situation is further complicated where the potential victim is also a client because failure to act to protect that client may amount to negligence. This type of dilemma may, for example, arise when working with an individual alone and also with their partner as a couple. Legal advice should be sought wherever necessary and circumstances permit.

In an emergency situation, where there is a real and imminent risk of serious harm, the potential victim may be warned, if they are unaware of the danger, or by informing others who are able to warn the victim, or informing the police to prevent immediate injury. The ethical dilemma is increased when a client is intending to inflict harm on another client, without letting one or both of them know that the other is receiving therapy. Bond and Mitchels (2008: 99) have developed a Disclosure Checklist, which has also been included below for reference in this section.

Checklist: Reporting criminal offences

Faced with a dilemma about whether to report a criminal offence, it might be helpful to consider these issues, preferably with the help of supervision or, if necessary, with other appropriate professional advice and help:

Q1 Does this constitute a criminal offence?
If yes, then go on to question 2.

Q2 Is this one of the offences where compulsory disclosure applies?
If yes, then the therapist must comply with the law
If no, then go on to question 3.

Q3 Is this an offence where disclosure is discretionary in law but is a defensible disclosure?

If yes, then consider the nature, seriousness and immediacy of the risk, the possible consequences of breach of confidentiality for the client and for the therapist, and the necessity and advisability of disclosure.

If no, then the issue of disclosure is discretionary for the therapist, but to do so may lead to a breach of the therapeutic contract and have other legal consequences, and so the risk to the client or others has to be balanced against the public interest, and the therapist's perception of the reality, seriousness and immediacy of the risk of harm to the client or others.

Checklist: Criminal activity – useful risk assessment questions

Where a client discloses criminal activity, if disclosure is discretionary, in addition to the issues set out earlier in this section, it may be helpful to consider:

- Was the offence committed in the past and now ended?
- Is the offence continuing now?
- Is this information about a planned future criminal offence?
- What is the nature of the risks to the client or to others?
- What is the nature and seriousness of the risk involved?
- How real and immediate are the risks?
- Is this client particularly vulnerable, or in need of protection from harm?
- Are others in need of immediate protection from harm?

5.3 I have heard about 'tipping off', but what is it?

Section 39 of the Terrorism Act 2000 creates an offence, colloquially known as 'tipping off', which, in relation to the investigation of terrorist activities, means disclosure of anything likely to prejudice the investigation or interference with material which is likely to prejudice the investigation. The courts take this seriously and the current maximum penalty for tipping off is five years' imprisonment, a fine or both.

Under s. 19 of that Act there is also a legal duty to disclose information to the appropriate authorities about certain uses of money to assist terrorist activities. The duty to under s. 19 arises where a person:

(a) believes or suspects that another person has committed an offence under any of sections 15 to 18, and

(b) bases his belief or suspicion on information which comes to his attention in the course of a trade, profession, business or employment.

(2) The person commits an offence if he does not disclose to a constable as soon as is reasonably practicable

(a) his belief or suspicion, and

(b) the information on which it is based.

Note: Section 15 relates to fundraising, s. 16 to the use of money or property, s. 17 to funding arrangements and s. 18 to money laundering.

The duty to report financial and property information learned at home was therefore not included in the Terrorism Act 2000. Although therapists are much less likely to receive this type of information than someone working in, say, banking or financial services, it is significant that the duty to inform does cover therapists where the information is acquired 'in the course of a trade, profession, business or employment'. There is a defence for an employee who has used a system established by his employer for making this type of report.

5.4 Whistle-blowing – what should I do if I discover that a colleague is negligent or unprofessional in their work, or has committed a crime that affects his work?

With the exception of the statutory requirements for disclosure (see 5.2.1), and the need to comply with common law and agency or organisational policies, there is no general duty to inform the police or relevant authorities if you find out that a colleague has committed a crime. However, as therapists, there are many professional and ethical issues for consideration here, such as the protection of clients, colleagues, the public and ourselves, and maintaining the standards of best practice within the profession. Employers, organisations and agencies may have rules applicable to this situation, requiring compliance as part of a therapist's contract. Several professional organisations have published guidance on 'whistle-blowing' procedures, for example the General Medical Council (GMC 2006: 43–5) provides:

> 43. You must protect patients from risk of harm posed by another colleague's conduct, performance or health. The safety of patients must come first at all times. If you have concerns that a colleague may not be fit to practise, you must take appropriate steps without delay, so that the concerns are investigated and patients protected where necessary. This means you must give an honest explanation of your concerns to an appropriate person from your employing or contracting body, and follow their procedures.

> 44. If there are no appropriate local systems, or local systems do not resolve the problem, and you are still concerned about the safety of patients, you should inform the relevant regulatory body. If you are not sure what to do, discuss your concerns with an impartial colleague or contact your defence body, a professional organisation, or the GMC for advice.

The British Psychological Society's *Professional Practice Guidelines for Counselling Psychologists* (2009) see www.bps.org.uk, para 1.2. 'Fitness to practise' provides that practitioners shall:

- continually monitor and maintain an effective level of personal functioning; i.e. should a practitioner feel unable to work effectively, he or she will seek advice from the supervisor or professional consultant. If necessary, the practitioner will withdraw for a time period considered appropriate;

- respond to concerns about the fitness of a colleague to practise safely. In order to safeguard both the client and the profession, they have a duty to discuss their concerns with their colleague or to share their concern with a senior colleague so that safe practice is maintained. The safety of the client is paramount; ...

We cannot provide any hard-and-fast rules in this situation, but recommend careful consideration of the issues and options, including any relevant agency and/or employment policies and guidance. We also recommend that self-employed therapists consider the issues, preferably with the help of supervision and, where appropriate, with professional or legal advice.

Checklist: Whistle-blowing

Where a therapist is aware that a colleague has committed an action which is a criminal offence, professional misconduct, or bad professional practice, a number of issues arise:

- What is the nature and severity of the colleague's action?
- Is the action a criminal offence?
- If you know of a criminal action, are you helping the criminal in some way or helping them to escape detection? If so, you too may be committing an offence.
- Does the action of the colleague impact in any way on their professional ability to do their job and does it have any impact on the profession generally?
- By keeping silent, in a professional context, are you putting yourself or any other people at risk?
- What do your agency policy, government and/or practice guidance, professional regulations and ethical framework require (or permit) you to do?
- Is there a risk of harm as a reprisal for disclosure? Would you, for example, need witness protection?

Many professions require disclosure by colleagues who become aware of malpractice and/or criminal matters which affect the practice standards of that profession. If possible, it is best to persuade the person concerned to acknowledge what they have done. If that is not possible then discuss the issues in supervision and if necessary seek legal or professional advice. Your professional insurance company helpline may be of assistance (see Chapter 6).

5.5 I was penalised for being late paying my tax last week, and last year I took part in a peace protest. Might these actions bring the profession into disrepute?

We cannot give any guidance on specific offences, but as a general rule the issue for professional governing bodies is whether the therapist's action will impact on the competence or professionalism of the individual therapist, or reflect badly on the profession as a whole. It also matters whether the action took place in the course of the therapist's work or was purely personal. For example, informal punishment for a peace protest or a minor financial irregularity entirely unconnected with therapy may have much less impact on the profession than the same action when directly related to clients or the workplace, or a conviction for a sexual offence or for an act of violence. The reason for the action may also be relevant. Some actions may be against the law (e.g. trespass) but taken for purely humanitarian purposes, such as a relatively minor offence committed in the course of peace activism.

5.6 My colleague was found guilty last year of downloading child pornography on his home computer. What are the professional consequences likely to be for him? Will he have to leave the profession?

An offence such as this is a serious crime. The therapist, if convicted, is likely to be put on the Sex Offenders Register and prevented from working with children (see 5.11). A professional body is likely to be concerned about that therapist's trustworthiness, professional competence and fitness to practice.

5.7 What if my clients bring drugs into the counselling premises or the therapy room without my knowledge? Would it be different if I did know?

We cannot deal with, or disclose, information of which we are unaware. However, there is the professional issue that therapists, particularly those working in high-risk situations, should put in place policies and procedures designed to avoid or minimise the risks to other clients and to themselves in the workplace. Not to do so may be considered reckless or negligent.

If a therapist *is* aware that clients are bringing illegal substances of any sort into the workplace and permits this to happen, or does nothing about it, this conduct might be considered to be unprofessional, particularly where the actions cause or increase physical risk to the client or others because, for example, the workplace involves careful use of hazardous chemicals or the operation of machinery. In addition to this, in some circumstances, if the therapist is an occupier of premises and if they have direct or implied knowledge of prohibited actions regarding illegal drugs (e.g. supplying a controlled drug or smoking or preparing certain controlled drugs contrary to s. 8 of the Misuse of Drugs Act 1971), they may be held criminally liable for the illegal activities. Suspicion is not knowledge, but knowledge may be inferred from shutting one's eyes to suspicious circumstances. The case of RV *Brock* and *Wyner* [2001] 1 WLR 1159, [2001] 2 Cr App R 745 held that, apart from knowledge, 'permits' involves an unwillingness to prevent the activity complained of, which can be inferred from failing to take reasonable steps to prevent it. What is reasonable is an objective test of fact for the jury. See also the cases of *R* v *Souter* [1971] 1 WLR 1187, 2ALL ER 1151 where the court held that 'permits' means 'with actual knowledge or shutting eyes to the obvious or allowing matters to go on without caring...'.

5.8 My 14 year-old client told me that her (much older) boyfriend got her drunk at a party and then had sex with her. What should I do?

The Sexual Offences Act 1956 (s. 1) creates the offence of rape of a woman or a man, and (s. 6) makes any sexual intercourse with a girl under the age of 16 illegal, but provides a defence for a man under the age of 24 who believes the girl to be over the age of 16. The law is different in Scotland, but sex with a girl under the age of 16 is still a criminal offence. Rape would undoubtedly be regarded as a serious crime, and therefore a defensible disclosure. The Department of Health offers the following guidance:

> Murder, manslaughter, rape, treason, kidnapping, child abuse or other cases where individuals have suffered serious harm may all warrant breaching confidentiality. Serious harm to the security of the state or to public order and crimes that involve substantial financial gain and loss will generally fall within this category. In contrast theft, fraud or damage to property where loss or damage is less substantial would generally not warrant breach of confidence. (DH 2003: 35)

It is also a criminal offence under s. 14 of the Sexual Offences Act 1956 for a man to make an indecent assault on a woman. The test of what constitutes an indecent assault is 'whether what occurred was so offensive to contemporary standards of modesty and privacy as to be indecent'. A defence is consent, but under that Act, a girl under the age of 16 cannot legally give her consent to such an act. However, there are certain statutory defences if the defendant believed the girl to be over 16 and that she consented.

Therapists who are asked by a young client to keep information confidential will have to consider a number of issues, including:

- the therapeutic issues involved
- why is the client telling the therapist about these events?
- the nature and seriousness of any criminal offence disclosed
- the age and capacity of the client to require confidentiality
- the balance of public interest in maintaining confidentiality and protection of the client or others.

See Chapter 4 at 4.7 for capacity and also Bond and Mitchels (2008: 21–2, 35–41, 99, and Chapter 11) for fuller discussion of confidentiality in the context of child protection, disclosure and capacity.

5.9 What exactly is harassment? If a former client harasses me, what can I do about it?

A person commits the offence of harassment when he pursues a course of conduct

(a) which amounts to harassment of another
(b) which he knows or ought to know amounts to harassment of another.

Two or more events can constitute a 'course of conduct', but the fewer the events or the greater their separation in time, the less likely it is that they will be so interpreted (see *Lau* v *DPP* [2000] 1 FLR 799 DC).

Under s. 1 of the Protection From Harassment Act 1997, harassment or putting people in fear of violence are criminal offences. In s. 3, civil remedies are also made available, including an injunction (a court order to prevent a course of action) and a warrant of arrest and/or damages for breach of an injunction. Harassment may take the form of violence, threats or lesser actions, for example repeated aggressive or pestering telephone calls. In the case of *Khorasandjian* v *Bush* [1993] 3 WLR 476 (Court of Appeal), the plaintiff, whose friendship with the defendant had broken down, claimed relief, alleging that the defendant had assaulted her, made threats of violence against her and pestered her with unwanted telephone calls to her parents' home. She said that he continued to behave aggressively towards her and, consequently, put her under great stress. The judge made an order restraining the defendant from 'using violence to, harassing, pestering or communicating with' the plaintiff. The defendant appealed the decision, but the Court of Appeal (Peter Gibson J. dissenting), held that:

- Harassment by unwanted telephone calls amounted to interference with the ordinary and reasonable enjoyment of property (and it did not matter that it was her parents home, and the plaintiff did not own it, as she had a right to live there).
- Verbal harassment which could not be strictly classified as a threat was actionable if it caused physical or psychiatric illness to the recipient, and where there was a risk that the cumulative effect of harassment might cause such illness, it could be restrained, and that, therefore, the grant of an injunction was justified to restrain the defendant's conduct as a whole.
- It was desirable that an injunction should be expressed in words which the person restrained could readily understand.

Racially aggravated harassment is an offence under s. 32, and if accompanied by violence, can be punished with imprisonment.

5.10 Professional consequences of criminal acts by therapists

The Criminal Records Bureau (CRB) is an executive agency of the Home Office which maintains the records of criminal offenders in the UK. Once a therapist is convicted of any criminal offence their criminal record will be held by the CRB. A search of the records is popularly known as a 'CRB check', which can require either 'Standard' or 'Enhanced' disclosure. A signed request for a CRB check contains the signatory's consent for disclosure. The 'Standard' CRB check will show details of convictions. The 'Enhanced' check shows not only convictions, but also acquittals and non-conviction information held on local police records relevant to the position which the person has selected. The police may also send additional information to employers in a separate letter. Agencies may require a certificated CRB check as a condition of employment.

5.11 Safeguarding children and vulnerable adults: the 'Vetting and Barring Scheme'

Risk management arrangements have been maintained in England and Wales under the framework of the Multi Agency Public Protection Arrangements (MAPPA). These include requirements for protective arrangements in certain areas of work ('regulated positions'), e.g. police, social services, probation services, health, housing, education, jobcentre plus, and people working with or with unsupervised access to children or vulnerable adults. Under the MAPPA framework, and supported by legislation, the government has maintained various lists of individuals (e.g. registered sex offenders, violent offenders and other offenders) who may pose various levels of risk (e.g. low, medium, high and very high). They are further categorised in relation to the potential subjects (e.g. children, vulnerable adults, etc.). Examples might include 'a sex offender posing a high risk to children' or 'a violent offender posing a medium risk to vulnerable adults'. In addition, certain people may be disqualified from working with children under a Disqualification Order made by a Crown Court on conviction for certain offences related to sex, drugs or violence. Government agencies also maintain further lists naming individuals deemed unsuitable for certain work.

More recently maintained lists include:

- 'List 99' (a list of those in respect of whom directions under s. 142 of the Education Act 2002 have been made)
- the 'Protection of Children Act List' (POCA List)
- the 'Protection of Vulnerable Adults List' (POVA List)
- Disqualification Orders made by a court under Part 2 of the Criminal Justice and Court Services Act 2000
- The Sex Offenders Register.

In addition, on completion of an application form giving the necessary details and consent plus the payment of a fee, the Criminal Records Bureau will issue a certificate (CRB Disclosure) providing information about an individual's criminal record, which may then be used to inform others about the suitability of that person to work with children or vulnerable adults. Therapists working with vulnerable groups in government departments and agencies may be required to obtain

CRB disclosure certificates and many other therapists and/or their employers have voluntarily applied for them, in order to provide a safety reassurance to their clients. In response to a deluge of applications by private individuals, restrictions were put in place and they now have to be made through certain agencies or an 'umbrella organisation' (for information, see www.crb.gov.uk).

There were certain problems with these various lists and disclosures. The lists were sometimes incomplete or inconsistent, and CRB disclosures can soon become out of date, even the day after the last search. In June 2004, the Report of the Bichard Inquiry into the Soham murders (available at: www.bichardinquiry. org.uk/) considered these problems and suggested that 'new arrangements should be introduced, requiring those who wish to work with children or vulnerable adults to be registered. The register would confirm that there is no known reason why an individual should not work with these clients' (Recommendation 19). This seemed to be a new departure with a different emphasis on positive preventive measures – to create and maintain a list of 'safe' people rather than all the existing (and sometimes confusing) lists. The government responded with new law creating a new central service, the Vetting and Barring Scheme, which is designed to assess risk, bar unsuitable people from working with children and vulnerable adults, and to impose safeguards to reduce the levels of risk in work with vulnerable groups.

5.11.1 The new Vetting and Barring Scheme

The *Safeguarding Vulnerable Groups Act 2006* (SVGA) underpins the Vetting and Barring Scheme, which is gradually being brought into force in England, Wales and Northern Ireland.

In Scotland, a similar Protecting Vulnerable Groups (PVG) Scheme is created by the Protection of Vulnerable Groups (Scotland) Act 2007, and goes live in 2010, with implementation phased in to minimise the administrative burden on individual organisations. For copy of the Protection of Vulnerable Groups (Scotland) see: www.posi.gov.uk/legislation/Scotland/acts2007/asp_20070014_en_1

For further details of the Scottish provisions, see the PVG Scheme Information Booklet (available online and in hard copy) and also available in BSL as a DVD, from jan.murray@scotland.gsi.gov.uk, or call the office on 0132 244 4907.

The Vetting and Barring Scheme in England, Wales and Northern Ireland

In England, Wales and Northern Ireland, the Vetting and Barring Scheme is implemented by the Independent Safeguarding Authority (ISA, see website www.isa.gov.org.uk). The ISA will maintain a list of individuals barred from working with children (the 'Child First' list) and another for those working with vulnerable adults (the 'Adult First' list). Inclusion on a list may happen automatically on caution or conviction for certain 'autobar' offences, or for meeting other specified criteria. Schedule 3 of the SVGA sets out the criteria for determining who is included on the lists, and the ISA makes decisions about inclusion. If a therapist feels that their name has been included in a list wrongly, then they may appeal against a finding of fact or on a point of law to the Care Standards Tribunal.

From 12 October 2009, the existing government maintained POVA and POCA lists will be replaced by new 'Adult First' and 'Child First' and individuals named on the lists are barred from regulated activity with children or adults. List 99 will be phased out by November 2010.

By 26 July 2010, all those covered by the legislation may voluntarily apply to be registered with the ISA. On and after 1 November 2010, everyone applying for new positions to whom the legislation applies must have ISA registration before they can start work, and there follows a period between 1 January 2010 and 2015 during which applications relating to existing roles will be phased in. For applicants taking part in controlled activities, registration begins in July 2014.

The details of the legislation can be found at: www.statutelaw.gov.uk and also www.opsi.gov.uk/acts/acts2006/ukpga_20060047_en_1, together with an explanatory note. See also the Safeguarding Vulnerable Groups Act 2006 (Commencement No 1) Order 2007 No 3545/2007, and the Safeguarding Vulnerable Groups (Northern Ireland) Order 2007 No 1351/2007, and www.dhsspsni.gov.uk/child_protection_guidance. Watch these websites for changes.

A child is generally defined in law as a person under the age of 18. Some of the regulated activities relate to children under the age of 16. A vulnerable adult is defined under s. 59 SVGA within the context of their situation or the services they receive, i.e.

- those in residential accommodation provided in connection with care or nursing or in receipt of domiciliary care services
- those receiving health care
- those in lawful custody or under the supervision of a probation officer
- those receiving a welfare service of a prescribed description or direct payments from a social services authority
- those receiving services, or taking part in activities, aimed at people with disabilities or special needs because of their age or state of health
- those who need assistance in the conduct of their affairs.

There are a number of ways in which a person's name might get onto one of the lists:

- automatic inclusion on caution or conviction for certain specified serious offences (with no right of appeal to the Care Standards Tribunal)
- automatic inclusion on caution or conviction for certain other specified offences (with a right of appeal to the Care Standards Tribunal)
- 'relevant conduct' which leads to inclusion (e.g. behaviour involving child pornography or violent pornography, harming or attempting to harm or inciting another to harm a child or vulnerable adult, or engaging in inappropriate sexual activity with a child or vulnerable adult, etc)
- the individual is judged by the ISA to pose a risk of harm to a child or vulnerable adult.

5.11.2 The potential impact of the Vetting and Barring Scheme on therapists

The law stated below applies to England, Wales and Northern Ireland. The law in Scotland is different and applies only where specifically stated.

A therapist who is cautioned for or convicted of any criminal offence specified in the criteria in the SVGA or who falls into any of the other categories for inclusion may now find their name entered on either or both of these lists. Depending on the nature of the criminal offence, they may or may not have a right of appeal against the inclusion of their name. It is not yet known how the Rehabilitation of Offenders legislation will be considered and implemented in the application of the ISA criteria. The ISA is likely to be providing guidance on this before implementation.

Therapists who are included on the barred 'Child First' list are prohibited from engaging in any 'regulated activity' which brings them into close contact with children, and those on the 'Adult First' list may not engage in any regulated activity with vulnerable adults (see Schedule 4), and this will include both paid and voluntary roles in a wide variety of settings.

Regulated activity

The term 'regulated activity' in relation to children is defined in SVGA Schedule 4 paras 1(1–2) and 2(1) to include activities 'carried out frequently' *or* where 'the period condition is satisfied'.

The ISA working definition of 'frequently' was once a month or more, but may soon change to once a week. The term 'intensively' is also used by the ISA and it is interpreted to mean the same as the 'period condition', defined in SVGA Part 3 Schedule 4 as activities carried out on 'more than two days' (i.e. three days or more) in any 30-day period, or overnight between 2am and 6am and which gives the person the opportunity to have face-to-face contact with children or vulnerable adults.

The term 'regulated activity' also includes activities carried out in any of the establishments listed in Schedule 4 para 3(1), i.e.:

- full-time educational institutions
- nursery education
- hospitals
- institutions for the detention of children
- children's homes
- childcare premises.

Childminding is also listed in para 1(3). Other functions are specifically listed in Schedule 4.

'Regulated activity' includes any form of work (whether for gain or not). The definition of 'activities' include any form of teaching, training or instruction of children, care or supervision of children, or advice or guidance for their physical, emotional or educational well-being. Therapists should also be aware of Schedule 4 para 2(d), which specifically refers to 'any form of treatment or therapy provided for a child'. Para 7(d) makes a similar provision in respect of adults. In view of the concern over internet abuse of vulnerable groups, it is also possible that the legislation will extend to include direct internet or email therapy with vulnerable groups either in this category or as 'controlled activity'.

Controlled activity

Beyond the level of regulated activity falls a further extended range of 'controlled activity' (defined in SVGA, s. 21). This is a wide sub-category covering those people who have 'an opportunity to have any form of contact with children' or who have 'access to the health records of children' SVGA, s. 21(9). Note that 'any form' would include direct and indirect contact.

If not falling within the regulated activities range, 'controlled activity' includes any form of health care, treatment or therapy which is carried out frequently or on three or more days in any 30-day period. This section gives a long list of controlled situations (including supervision and management). These include situations where individuals have access to sensitive records about children and vulnerable adults, e.g. education and social services records, Children and Family Courts Advisory Service (CAFCASS) records, etc. For a description of the role of CAFCASS see Glossary. It also refers to any health care, treatment or therapy provided under statutory arrangements.

Section 22 defines controlled activity in relation to adults. The provisions are similar, and the list includes primary care, hospital care, domiciliary care and community care services, with an opportunity to have any form of contact with a vulnerable adult, or access to their health or social services records, or other prescribed information about them.

The Secretary of State may make regulations relating to controlled activity, and the circumstances in which a responsible person may (or may not) permit another to engage in controlled activity (SVGA, s. 23). Failure to comply may constitute a criminal offence. There may, therefore, be some non-regulated but controlled activities in which those people on the barred lists may engage, but where safeguards must be put in place by employers (and others with responsibility to manage the controlled activity) to manage the risks.

All therapists working closely with children or vulnerable adults, whether as volunteers, on a self-employed basis, or in employment, if they are engaging in 'regulated activity' must comply with the legislation and unless they are barred, they must apply to be 'subject to monitoring' (see SVGA, s. 24). Some therapists may find themselves in 'controlled activity' situations which are also subject to regulation. The SVGA applies not only to therapy, but includes other activities, e.g. school governors, educational board trustees, etc.

Under the new legislation, failure to comply with monitoring requirements, or using a barred person to carry out any regulated activity may constitute a criminal offence. Managers and directors of companies and partners in businesses are potentially liable for the actions of their organisation. Therapists in employment or who are in partnership may therefore find themselves liable for any non-compliance with the SVGA.

There is an exception in s. 58 of the Safeguarding Vulnerable Groups Act 2006 for activities carried out in 'family relationships', i.e. between two people who live in the same household and treat each other as members of the same family, and 'in the course of a personal relationship between or among friends for no commercial consideration'. Such exceptions allow, for example, a person to carry out a regulated or controlled activity without a monitoring requirement, such as looking after a grandchild, or looking after an elderly and vulnerable neighbour who is a friend. Regulations will more closely define these terms and exceptions, but note that child protection and other protective legislation still applies where relevant.

In Wales, a person barred as a result of an autobar conviction or caution will not be able to work or volunteer in controlled activity in Wales. In England and Northern Ireland, barred people may be able to undertake controlled activities with tough safeguards, such as stringent supervision. For Scotland, please see the websites in 5.11.1 for details as the new legislation and guidance unfold.

Monitoring procedures and safeguards

The monitoring procedure includes a Criminal Records Bureau check and enquires of local police forces. Employers, agencies and private therapists can arrange a CRB check, directly or through an 'umbrella' organisation, which will, on payment of a fee, provide the necessary documentation, process the check and forward on the results. In England and Wales, for details of the process and for news of any future changes, see the CRB home page at www.crb.gov.uk/. In Scotland, the Central Registered Body in Scotland (CRBS) provides enhanced disclosures in the voluntary sector for those working with children, young people and adults at risk, see www.crbs.org.uk. Disclosure Scotland provides disclosures upon request and payment of a fee, see www.disclosure Scotland.co.uk/apply/. In Northern Ireland, a similar service is provided by Access Northern Ireland, see www.accessni.gov.uk/.

Information may also be gathered from other sources, for example, schools, local authorities, professional bodies and supervisory authorities, and then passed to the ISA, which may impose barring. The therapist would have a right of making representations or appeal, save in the most serious cases. This requirement for the ISA to receive and assess information also implies a concomitant duty on local authorities and others to provide it. The searches and enquiries are to be repeated at intervals.

There are situations where CRB checks continue to be necessary and appropriate, and they should continue to be carried out regularly, as would normally be appropriate for the company, agency, or organization. Seek advice from the CRB, Disclosure Scotland, Access Northern Ireland or ISA if in any doubt.

From 12 October 2009, employers and managers of volunteers in agencies and organisations working with vulnerable groups have a duty to ensure compliance with the new law by all relevant staff and volunteers. This duty includes referral to the ISA of dismissals for conduct which has harmed or poses a risk of harm to children or vulnerable adults. There are criminal penalties for non-compliance. If you need more information about the duty to refer, contact the Independent Safeguarding Authority at the address below.

If your name was on the POVA or POCA Lists, on 12 October 2009 it was be transferred on to the relevant Adults or Children's Barred Lists, and you will then be barred from 'regulated activities'.

If your work is defined as a regulated activity or controlled activity in the SVGA, and/or if you work with children or vulnerable adults frequently (once a month or more), or for three days or more in each 30 days, and/or in some cases overnight between 2am and 6am, the new procedures under the Safeguarding Vulnerable Groups Act 2006 are likely to apply to you, and where appropriate, from 26 July 2010, you may request voluntary ISA registration. Forms are available from the ISA (see the address and website below). There will be a flat fee, currently set at £64 per application.

From 1 November 2010 onwards, everyone to whom the new law applies, and who is taking on a new post involving regulated activity, will be obliged to obtain ISA registration before starting work.

From 1 January 2011, there begins a phased process in which everyone to whom the legislation applies must register – if this may apply to you, check with the ISA.

From July 2014, all applicants taking part in controlled activity must register.

There are criminal penalties for non-compliance with the duty of referral and the Vetting and Barring procedures. If you think that you may have a duty to make a referral, you can write to the Independent Safeguarding Authority, PO Box 181, Darlington DL1 9FA.

If you are concerned to know whether the legislation applies to you or to your work, or when to apply for registration, you can call the ISA Contact Centre on 0300 1231111 between 8am and 5.30pm, or visit www.isa-gov.org.uk for further information. The resource library on the ISA website has downloadable information documents. Your employer, agency, local authority legal services or a lawyer may also help you to consider whether you (or your employer or managing body) will need to comply with the monitoring process. The vetting and barring practice and procedure is still in the process of development. Watch the press and these websites for more information about procedures and changes as they develop.

Therapists in Scotland should see www.opsi.gov.uk/legislation/scotland/acts2007/asp_20070014_en_1 for the statute, and for further details of the Scottish provision, see the PVG Scheme Information Booklet (available online and in hard copy) and also available in BSL as a DVD from jan.murray@scotland/gsi.gov.uk, or call the office on 0131 244 4907.

All therapists in private practice who have direct or unsupervised contact with children and/or vulnerable adults would be well advised to check with the ISA as to whether (and when) vetting and barring compliance is required, and/or whether a voluntary request for a criminal records check continues to be appropriate. Voluntary compliance is reassuring to clients and their carers, and complies with the 'soft law' of government and best practice guidance (see Introduction and Chapter 1).

Employers, agencies and private therapists can, at the moment, arrange a CRB check directly or through an 'umbrella' organisation, which will, on payment of a fee, provide the necessary documentation, process the check and forward on the results. For details of the process, and any future changes, see the CRB home page at www.crb.gov.uk/. Disclosure Scotland at www.disclosurescotland.co.uk, or www.accessni.gov.uk.

Some contracts of employment may contain conditions about criminal convictions or criminal activity where it is considered potentially detrimental in any way to best therapy practice, to the profession, or to the employer or agency. Professional organisations usually impose conditions of membership designed to maintain the good standing of the profession. Judgement about whether certain convictions are relevant or detrimental to good therapy practice or to the profession is a matter for a decision in each individual case, and if in doubt, legal and/or professional advice should be sought.

Where a criminal case is pending against a therapist (i.e. there is as yet no conviction), in law the therapist is deemed to be innocent until proven guilty (or until they plead guilty), but there may be contractual conditions of employment which require suspension of their work pending the outcome of the criminal trial. It is not yet known how pending criminal trials (cases *sub judice*) or the rehabilitation of offenders legislation will impact upon the ISA or PVG criteria. Further government guidance is anticipated which will clarify interpretation of the legislation.

In cases where children are at risk, Part 1 of *Working Together to Safeguard Children* (DFES 2006c) – statutory guidance issued under s. 7 of the Local Authority Social Services Act 1970 – must be complied with by local authorities carrying out their social services functions. Part 2 is non-statutory practice guidance. *Working Together to Safeguard Children* represents a standard of good practice for all organisations. For example, managers and staff in educational institutions and those in organisations and agencies with a duty to safeguard and promote the welfare of children under s.11 of the Children Act 2004 are encouraged to follow it, together with the guidance on that duty (see: www.everychildmatters.gov.uk/socialcare/safeguarding). Therefore, therapists who train or supervise others, or who work with colleagues or clients to whom any of these lists or protective orders may apply, should pay attention to the guidance set out in Chapter 12 of the *Working Together to Safeguard Children* (DfES 2006c). For child protection law, see Mitchels (2009). References for guidance from the Scottish Executive on child protection can be found at the end of the book.

6 Professional Indemnity and Other Insurance

There are relatively few court cases against therapists. Do I really need to have professional indemnity insurance?

What sort of events might be covered by professional indemnity insurance?

Is it worth shopping around for insurers and what should I look for?

What will professional indemnity insurance policies not cover?

How can I protect myself from the costs of defending a claim made against me?

Do I have to have employer's liability insurance if I have any employees?

Will professional indemnity insurance be refused if I have had a complaint made against me in the past?

6.1 Why do I need to insure?

The law does not at the moment specifically require therapists to have professional indemnity insurance cover, and it is true that there are relatively few court cases against therapists, but court cases are very expensive, public funding is limited, and none of us have immunity from the law. There are considerable numbers of complaints about therapists to their professional bodies each year, and responding to complaints can be time-consuming and expensive. Often, complaints involve the law and legal assistance is required. Government regulation of the profession is probably imminent and will almost certainly require compulsory insurance cover. Professional bodies (e.g. BACP, UKCP and BPC) recommend insurance in their practice guidance and some, including BACP, require cover as a precondition of accreditation. Insurance is a means of providing a level of protection for the profession, clients and the public interest, and it is our firm view that adequate professional insurance cover is essential for all those in therapeutic practice.

When looking for professional insurance cover, most people seem to consider mainly the cost, so advertisements offer cheap premiums, but often inexpensive insurers provide only minimum cover. Don't be tempted by a cheap deal, thinking that insurance is only in place because our professional organisation requires it. We never know when we might need to claim, and it is only then that insurance is really tested, so we should evaluate insurance by how well it will meet our individual needs and how quickly and efficiently it will perform when a claim has to be made.

This chapter looks at the types of professional insurance cover that we may need and the issues to consider when looking for insurance cover and making insurance arrangements.

6.2 Professional insurance cover

6.2.1 Premises

Bear in mind that the provision of therapy is regarded in law as a business (see Chapters 8 and 9). We consider the use of different types of premises for the provision of therapy in Chapter 7. Therapists working from premises owned or managed by someone else, e.g. the organisation or agency with which they work, should check that the premises are fully insured against public liability to clients, visitors, employees, volunteers and others. Therapists should also ensure that the policy is not invalidated by conducting a therapy business on the premises.

Therapists working from their own premises, whether leased, owned or rented, have a responsibility to provide professional liability insurance cover for their clients and for their work.

Where premises are leased or rented, under the terms of the lease or tenancy agreement the landlord may have responsibility to provide insurance cover for the building, maintenance, accidental damage, and public liability. Check that the landlord's insurance policy and the terms of the lease or tenancy agreements are all compatible with running a therapy business from the premises, and that there are no exclusion clauses which prohibit or restrict your particular business use of the premises. Often, for example, where part of a private home is used for business, the insurers of the buildings and contents may allow the business use (but sometimes not, you should always check with them) and will sometimes cover any office and other equipment used for the business, but will almost always exclude cover for theft or malicious damage caused by business visitors and any business liabilities (however, the therapist's professional liability insurance should provide cover for this and the insurers might be able to suggest alternative solutions to any property insurance problems).

If you own the premises from which you work, review the insurance cover for:

- the fabric, construction and maintenance of the building
- accidental damage to the premises
- theft and non-accidental damage
- public liability.

Ensure that any exclusion clauses in the insurance policy for the building and contents are compatible with the provision of therapy as a business on the premises. It may be that two policies may be necessary, one for the building and contents and another to cover the therapy business. In this case, make sure that all possible liabilities are covered.

6.2.2 Life and health insurances and income protection

If you rely on work for an income and are unable to work for any reason, the purchase of necessities, payment of debts, bills and family care may suffer. Policies are available which provide life insurance, i.e. payment on the event of death, or health insurance, i.e. to provide an income if health is temporarily or permanently impaired. The cost of life and health insurance is usually linked to the level of cover and the sums payable in the event of a claim. Choosing the right one is a balance between what is necessary, practicable and affordable.

Income protection insurance will provide a level of income during a period of illness or incapacity.

6.2.3 Professional indemnity and public liability insurance

Insurance for professional indemnity, including public liability cover where appropriate, is a requirement of most professional organisations and, although not yet required for therapists by law or regulation, we regard professional indemnity insurance cover as a professional responsibility for all therapists.

Some employers provide an indemnity for their employees acting in the course of their employment. Private cover is useful, even when employed, since some claims may involve conflicts of interest or disputes with the employer. In other circumstances, organisations and agencies require therapists to arrange their own insurance cover as a condition of their working.

Ask whether your insurers provide:

- advice and assistance in dealing with professional complaints
- legal assistance in responding to complaints and legal claims
- a telephone helpline for advice and assistance or access to other help and resources

and cover for:

- claims for negligence
- dealing with allegations of professional misconduct
- claims for libel and slander
- claims for breach of the therapeutic contract
- public liability
- legal fees in dealing with complaints and claims.

Additional cover may include:

- directors' and officers' liability
- public relations assistance to mitigate damage to reputation
- assistance with criminal defence.

6.3 Finding the right insurance provider

Some useful guidelines when searching for the right insurance provider are listed here:

- Look for a specialist insurer who understands what you do
- Ask for a range of quotes
- Ask exactly what is covered by each quote – and compare with the lists in 6.2
- Ask what is *not* covered – and refer to 6.2 and 6.4
- Look at limits of indemnity – and refer to 6.4
- Compare the quotes from different providers on a 'like for like' basis
- Remember that insurance proves its worth when you have to make a claim.

6.4 Limits of indemnity, exclusion clauses and policy restrictions

6.4.1 Limits of indemnity

Most insurance companies set a *limit of indemnity*, i.e. a limit on the total amount of money they would pay out on each policy. This will usually be expressed as indemnity 'for any one claim' or indemnity 'in the aggregate' or similar words to this effect. There is a vast difference. Response to even one claim may take a good deal of money, for example, cover of £1 million might soon be used up. Cover for 'any one claim' is best, in that the stated limit applies to each separate claim on the policy in one insurance year. Cover 'in the aggregate' means that the limit applies to all claims in that year, taken together, so if more than one claim arose in a year, there is a risk that the total of all the claims might exceed the limit.

6.4.2 Policy restrictions and exclusion clauses

Some insurance companies impose limits on claims in various ways. For professional indemnity it is unusual to restrict the number of possible claims in one year, but watch for the hidden limit of indemnity cover 'in the aggregate' explained above.

Some insurers impose an 'excess' at various levels. Usually, the higher the excess, the lower is the insurance premium. In other words, the insurer will only pay out on claims that exceed a certain level, the insured having to foot the bill for the 'excess' amount. An excess of £500 would mean that the insurer pays out on claims that exceed this amount, with the insured therapist paying the first £500 themselves.

Ask for a copy of the terms and conditions of the policy *before* taking it on, and read all the exclusion clauses, particularly those that appear in 'small print' and in less obvious parts of the policy documents. Make sure that the exclusions set out do not compromise the cover that you want to achieve. For example, some policies may exclude certain working environments, e.g. the therapist's or client's home, or certain therapeutic or mediation activities.

When changing insurers, watch out for the exclusion of claims arising from past events when the insured was covered by another insurer. Look for retroactive cover, provided automatically under a claims made policy or sometimes as an extension to an occurrence based policy (see 6.6 below).

6.5 Factors that might affect the cost of insurance

- Extent of cover (see 6.2)
- Level of cover (limit of indemnity) (see 6.4)
- Whether the policy provides 'aggregate' or 'for any one claim' cover (see 6.4.1)
- Insured's liability for 'excess' payments (see 6.4.2)
- Exclusions (see 6.4.2)
- Period of cover (whether 'claims made' or 'occurrence' policy – does it provide retroactive cover?) (see 6.4.2 and 6.6).

Remember that some things may be negotiable. Work out what extent and level of cover is required beforehand, and then don't be afraid to ask whether the policy can be altered to suit your needs. Insurers may be able to provide advice and help on the appropriate levels of cover in relation to workload, place of work and identified risks. Insurers may well be able to negotiate the terms and conditions to meet a therapist's specific identified needs.

6.6 What to watch for when changing insurers

Claims against therapists may stem from recent events or they may arise from events that happened many years in the past. When changing insurers, be clear about what is actually covered by the new policy. Cover starts from the date of the new policy, but what does it mean to say 'cover starts...'?

Some insurers provide policy cover on an 'occurrence' basis, i.e. the policy is triggered by the date on which the event occurred and therefore (unless there is a retroactive extension clause) such policies exclude claims arising from events occurring in the past when the therapist might have been covered by a different insurer. In this situation, if a claim is made, the therapist would have to go back to the insurer they used at the time the event took place and lodge a claim with them. There is a risk that the old insurer may no longer exist, or that the old cover which applied years before may no longer be adequate or that the previous policy might have been a 'claims made' policy. An occurrence-based policy will only give cover for claims that arise from earlier events if it has a retroactive extension clause. Some non-specialist insurers might not have one.

Other insurers offer policies on a 'claims made' basis, which means that it is the policy which is in force at the time the claim is made against the therapist that responds to the claim, not the one, if any, that might have been in force at the time the event took place. Claims made policies automatically provide this 'retroactive cover', meaning that the new insurer will cover the therapist for complaints and claims made after the date that the new policy began, no matter how far in the past the events occurred that caused the claim. Some non-specialist insurers might seek to impose a retroactive restriction date (usually the inception date of the policy) on a claims made policy but, usually, only where there is no previous insurance history.

6.7 What risks do I need to insure against?

In general, insurance cover should be considered for:

- the premises (to include reconstruction cost in the event of total loss)
- the maintenance and decoration of the premises
- contents of the premises
- public liability
- the health and life of the therapist (with income protection if necessary)
- professional indemnity.

6.8 Useful tips when arranging insurance

Read the terms and conditions of the policy carefully *before* agreeing to the insurance contract. In particular, notice the cover offered and the exclusion clauses. If there are terms which are unsuitable, raise these with the insurers and negotiate.

If a policy has exclusion clauses which affect the cover required for your practice (e.g. in relation to working from home), do not accept the policy. Negotiate for specific cover or search for another insurer.

Bear in mind that although some insurers offer comprehensive cover, in most cases, more than one policy may be necessary to give the cover required, e.g. one for the premises, one for professional practice, and another for health and life cover, etc.

The most important thing is to be completely open and honest with the insurance company. A policy may be invalidated if it is found that information has been deliberately withheld or the wrong information has been given, e.g. failing to declare a previous conviction or a professional complaint (see 6.10 below).

6.9 Employer's liability insurance

Under the Employer's Liability (Compulsory Insurance) Act 1969, s. 1(1): 'Every employer carrying on business in Great Britain shall insure and maintain insurance against liability for bodily injury or disease sustained by his employees, and arising out of or in the course of that employment...' There must be 'an approved policy' under EEC Regulation E13020 (a policy without certain exceptions or conditions) issued by an authorised insurer (Insurance Companies (Amendment) Regulations 1992). The minimum cover required is £5 million for any one or more of the employees arising out of any one occurrence, under regulation 3(1) of the Employer's Liability (Compulsory Insurance) Regulations 1998. A certificate of insurance must be displayed in the workplace (or can now be made electronically). Failure to do so is a criminal offence, with a £1,000 fine.

For the definition of employment, and the responsibilities of therapists as employers or employees, see Chapter 9. While it is fairly unlikely that a therapist or their employees might sustain bodily injury at work, it is still a possibility. We may, for example, be attacked by a dangerous client, made ill by carbon monoxide or asbestos in the roof, or be injured by a falling shelf in the office.

Certain employers are exempt from the regulations, including nationalised industries, health service bodies and National Health Trusts. Under the Employer's Liability (Compulsory Insurance) Act 1969, s. 2(2)(a), certain employees are exempt, including family members: spouse, father, mother, son, daughter or other close relatives. An exemption now also applies for Limited Liability Companies that have only one employee where that employee is the owner of the business.

6.10 Will professional indemnity insurance be refused if I have had a complaint made against me in the past?

As we have seen earlier in this chapter, when applying for insurance cover, it is important to be honest about matters which may affect the nature or the level of the cover provided. Failure to be honest may invalidate the contract of insurance and leave the therapist without cover (see Chapter 4 for contracts).

Insurers take into account the level of potential risk when they consider cover and calculate premiums. Usually there is a question on the proposal form (or asked during a telephone application) about whether the therapist has been the subject of any past complaints or whether the therapist is aware of any circumstances which might give rise to a complaint. These questions must be answered honestly. Usually, insurers will be willing to provide cover to someone who has been the subject of a complaint, but they may ask further questions about the circumstances, the decisions of any disciplinary proceedings, and any remedial action taken (e.g. retraining) in order to assess the present level of risk. Insurers are likely to charge an increased premium if the level of risk is considered to be higher than average.

Insurers may refuse future cover if the level of risk to the client is considered so high that it is professionally unacceptable or in situations where the provision of insurance would not be cost-effective.

Our view is that in all insurance proposals, honesty is the best policy. Good insurance gives peace of mind. The potential risks to both client and therapist of working without adequate insurance cover are professionally unacceptable.

7 Legal Responsibilities and Liabilities as an Owner or Occupier of Premises

My counselling room is up three flights of stairs with no lift. Am I breaking the law relating to disability?

What would happen if a client tripped on my carpet and hurt themselves?

If I work from home, do I need to have a first aid kit and fire doors?

Do I need planning consent to make a counselling room in the garden?

I own my house and live in a quiet street. Can my neighbours stop me from working from home?

What are the possible consequences if I start using my home as a place of business?

What are the pros and cons of taking on a business lease or tenancy?

The topics in this chapter each involve huge areas of complex law and in this book we cannot venture into detail, but we will address the questions that we are asked most often by therapists. We will explore what a responsible practitioner might do to minimise the risks to their practice, their clients and themselves. We provide a framework for thinking around the topics, with pointers indicating where further information can be found when necessary.

7.1 Disability discrimination legislation compliance

This chapter is about facilities and premises. We cover the rights of disabled therapists in the context of employment in Chapter 9 at 9.6.1. We consider here the disability rights of therapists and clients and indicate helpful resources.

The Disability Discrimination Act 1995 (DDA 1995) was extended by the Disability Discrimination Act 2005 (DDA 2005). The Equality and Human Rights Commission runs a dedicated disability helpline (see Useful Resources at the end of this book), and the Acts and guidance are available on their website (www. direct.gov.uk/en/DisabledPeople/RightsAndObligations/DisabilityRights/DG_ 4001068; Braille, Audio, BSL and Easy read versions are available from The Stationery Office at www.tsoshop.co.uk/parliament/bookstore.asp?AF=A10075& FO=1160903&DI=551113).

Disability is defined in s. 1(1) of the DDA 1995, subject to the provisions of Schedule 1, as 'a person who has a physical or mental impairment that has a substantial and long term adverse effect on his ability to carry out normal day-to-day activities'. The effect of an impairment is long term if it has lasted at least 12 months, or if it is likely to last at least that long, or for the rest of the person's life, or if it is likely to recur if in remission (DDA 1995, Sch 1, paras 2(1) and (2)).

Under the DDA 1995, Sch 1, para 4(1), an impairment is taken to be likely to affect ability to carry out normal day-to-day functioning only if it affects one of the following:

(a) mobility
(b) manual dexterity
(c) physical co-ordination
(d) continence
(e) the ability to lift, carry or otherwise move everyday objects
(f) speech, hearing or eyesight
(g) memory or ability to concentrate, learn or understand or
(h) the perception of physical danger.

The definition includes people with HIV, cancer and multiple sclerosis from the point of diagnosis. Under the Acts, disabled people have statutory rights in employment, goods, services, buying and renting property, and public functions.

Therapists, whether providing paid or free-of-charge therapy, are providing services in the context of a 'profession or trade'. Part III of the DDA 1995 makes it unlawful to discriminate against a disabled person by unjustifiably providing less favourable treatment (s. 20) or failing to take reasonable steps to provide access or facilities (s. 21). Government agencies and large businesses have strict rules for compliance. For smaller agencies and businesses, see *Making Access to Goods and Services Easier for the Disabled: A Practical Guide for Small Business and Service Providers*, by the Disability Rights Commission, which is available from the Equality and Human Rights Commission or at www.direct.gov.uk/en/DisabledPeople/Everydaylifeandaccess/Everydayaccess/DG_4018353.

7.1.1 My counselling room is up three flights of stairs with no lift – am I breaking the law?

The DDA 1995 only requires service providers to make reasonable provisions. In the case of a small business, factors to consider include efficacy, practicality, cost, the disruption of making changes, the extent of resources available, and the availability of financial or other assistance.

The therapist should explore the possibility of making any necessary DDA changes and evaluate the options available, for example, the possibility of moving to other premises, obtaining grants or undertaking necessary work (e.g. constructing ramps, widening doors, providing extra facilities, etc.). The research should indicate potential cost, disruption, practicality and the feasibility of compliance. From this the therapist can then gain an idea of whether they could reasonably be required to make the changes. Seek advice from the Equality and Human Rights Commission Disability Helpline, and their publications (see Useful Resources). As an alternative to making changes to premises for disabled clients, there may be creative responses to meet the need, such as the use of alternative rooms in another building with disability access on certain days. Other facilities may be easier to provide, for example, large print, audio, Braille or BSL video information about therapy services.

An audit of the premises and the feasibility of making disability provisions can be obtained from the Centre for Accessible Environment (www.cae.org.uk) or the National Register of Access Consultants (www.nrac.org.uk). For their contact details, see Useful Resources.

7.2 Health and safety

Public liability insurance may cover a claim by a client who trips and sustains accidental injury (see Chapter 6), but there is a responsibility on employers and/or those who are in total or partial control of work premises to provide a safe environment for:

- employees
- staff and volunteers
- clients, customers and those who use the facilities
- visitors
- neighbours
- the Public
- trespassers (in some cases).

Relevant legislation includes:

- Health and Safety at Work Act 1974
- Regulatory Reform (Fire Safety) Order 2005
- Occupiers Liability Acts 1957 and 1984
- Control of Asbestos Regulations 2006.

Detailed information can be found in the legislation and in resource books such as *The Health and Safety at Work Handbook* (Bamber et al. 2008). Perhaps the most important piece of legislation is the Health and Safety at Work Act 1974, which provides that an employer with five or more employees must prepare a written Health and Safety Policy Statement, and the arrangements and organisation for carrying it out, and bring it to the attention of employees. Those who are self-employed must take similar care of themselves under the legislation. Employees must co-operate with statutory duties and also take reasonable care of themselves and others.

Under the various pieces of legislation, risks to be considered include:

- fire
- asbestos and other dangerous substances in the building

- access to premises
- equipment
- activities
- accidents and emergencies.

Action taken to minimise risks may include:

- assessment of client (customer) needs and abilities
- maintenance of safe access
- fire prevention and control
- first aid facilities and training
- information, training and instruction
- supervision and control
- monitoring
- emergency arrangements.

Therapists working in agencies, organisations or shared premises should ensure that they obtain information about compliance with the requirements of the Health and Safety at Work Act. The local authority has a Health and Safety Officer who may be willing to advise.

Therapists working from home, who use a room in their house from time to time for therapy (and therefore do not have a part of the house designated solely for their work) and who have no employees, although perhaps not required to comply with the Health and Safety at Work Act, should be aware of (and insure against) the possible risks to clients and themselves, and bear in mind the general duty of care to clients (and visitors) and take reasonable safety measures, e.g. adequate household fire safety precautions, removal of dangerous substances and keeping a first aid kit available. There is always a possibility in any of our lives that family, clients or visitors may need first aid, and basic first aid training is always useful.

7.3 Public liability

In Chapter 6 we discussed public liability insurance. The Health and Safety legislation (see 7.2 above) aims to ensure that the environment provided is as safe as possible. However, accidents or unforeseen events can happen, e.g. an attack by a client on another person, or a client falling over a carpet or stairs. Public liability insurance cover is necessary to protect therapists, clients and the public in the event of an accident in which a member of the public suffers personal injury.

7.4 Planning regulations and restrictive covenants

Where a therapist owns the premises within which they work, the premises may be subject to restrictive covenants and also to the national and local planning law.

7.4.1 Restrictive covenants

These are restrictions placed by agreement on the use of buildings and land, usually entered into for the benefit of neighbours and the community at the time that the land was sold or the building constructed, and they are set out in title deeds and leases. In titles that are registered with the Land Registry, restrictive covenants are entered on the register along with the title to the land, and a copy can be obtained for the payment of a fee from the local Land Registry.

Often the same restrictions will apply to a group of buildings or dwellings. There may be covenants against the construction of fences, sheds or garages, perhaps to preserve a view or to maintain a common style.

Frequently, covenants limit the use of the property to prevent nuisance to neighbours. For example, many dwelling houses and flats have restrictive covenants forbidding certain uses of the premises (a covenant against business use may prohibit 'any business', or prohibit specific sorts of business, e.g. use of the building as a shop or garage, etc.). A covenant against business use may mean that neighbours could object if the therapist begins to work from home, and action could be taken in the local county court to enforce the restrictive covenant.

Once restrictive covenants exist, they are difficult to remove. Seek advice from a conveyancing lawyer.

7.4.2 Planning law

Even though we may own premises, we cannot always do what we like with them. In the public interest, sometimes limits are imposed by statute and regulations on building, the use of the premises, development and alterations, etc. This is a huge area of law, and when considering whether planning consent is required, a useful resource is the Planning Portal, a UK government online planning and building regulations resource, available at: www.planningportal.gov.uk.

This resource provides the law, forms and guidance. It was designed to help enquirers to find out whether their proposed action requires planning consent, the relevant building regulations that apply, and to enable them to make any necessary application.

If you are considering changing the use of home to business, seek legal advice because the change of use may not only involve permissions but it may have longer-term tax implications (see Chapter 8).

7.5 Use of home for business

Working from home can be very convenient, but it has its potential problems. We have discussed health and safety at 7.2, planning and land law issues at 7.4, leases and tenancies at 7.6, duty of care in Chapter 3 and insurance in Chapter 6. Working from home may raise ethical issues, however, since the use of the premises may be shared with the therapist and also with their family, pets and general bric a brac, all of which may provide (often quite unintentionally) challenges for clients. Such challenges may include being licked enthusiastically or jumped upon by the dog as they come through the gate, unexpected encounters with family members or the cat in the hall, or being faced with family pictures, religious objects, or other things which may constitute unwelcome self-disclosure. The insurance companies report complaints and claims based on issues just such as these. We have also heard of situations where clients felt uncertain about whether they had privacy, including a therapist allegedly keeping a pair of large male boots prominently displayed in the porch to prevent clients assuming that she was alone in the house.

Check whether a home that is mortgaged has any clauses imposed by the mortgagee which restrict the use of the property. Check, too, for any restrictive covenants and planning restrictions in title deeds, leases and tenancies which may prohibit business use of the premises. Seek legal advice where necessary.

Check the terms of the building and contents insurance policy. Arrange insurance to cover necessary aspects of the therapy business at home (for discussion and checklists, see Chapter 6).

Issues to consider when setting up business at home include the following:

- If renting or leasing, do I need the landlord's consent?
- Are there any restrictive covenants? (see 7.4)
- Do I need planning consent? (see 7.4)
- Insurance (see Chapter 6 generally, and at 6.7)
- Health and safety (see 7.2)
- Disability legislation compliance (see 7.1)
- Financial, mortgage and tax issues (see Chapter 8)
- Data protection compliance where relevant
- Ethical and, in particular, boundary issues, e.g. confidentiality for the client on arrival and leaving or waiting, use of therapy room, storage of client records, facilities, inadvertent self-disclosure by the therapist through their possessions in the home, etc. (See the following BACP Information Sheets: E1 – Gabriel and Casemore 2008; Bond and Jenkins 2008; G2 – Bond et al. 2009; G3 – Jacobs 2007; G5 – Jackson 2003; P1 – Moore 2005; P2 – Dale 2008b; and P11 – Dale 2008a.)

7.6 Ownership of land, leases and tenancies

The person who owns land or property outright is the 'freeholder'. Subject to the law, the freeholder may sell, give away, or dispose of all or any part of their land as they wish. Some property is owned subject to commercial or family arrangements, e.g. trusts, or to conditions of use (see restrictive covenants at 7.4). Freehold and leasehold titles to land are proved by lawyers through the 'title deeds', e.g. conveyances, leases etc., and title may be registered with the Land Registry. New titles should now be registered. For information about registration, see www.landregistry.gov.uk.

A lease is an agreement between the owner of the property ('head lessor' or 'lessor') to allow the 'lessee' to occupy a property for a specific term of years. A sum of money ('premium') may be required by the lessor for granting the lease. The lessee pays the premium to buy the legal right to the tenancy of the premises for a fixed number of years. The term remaining on a lease will gradually decrease over time, and concomitantly, its value. Leases can be bought and sold, like any other property rights, and for guidance see the *Code of Practice for Commercial Leases*, (British Property Federation, 2002) which can be obtained from the website www.commercialleasecodeew.co.uk. Guidance as to 'model clauses', i.e. fair clauses between landlord and tenant for use in commercial leases is provided by the British Property Federation and the British Council of Offices (2007) and is available from www.bpf.org.uk/publications.

A lessee ('tenant') may, with the consent of the head lessor (for which a payment and indemnity for legal fees may be required), 'assign' occupation of all or part of the premises to another person (a 'sub-lessee' or 'sub-tenant'), e.g. the lessee of business premises holding a 10 year lease may allow a therapist to use all or part of the premises for a period of five years.

Apart from leases, there are other forms of tenancy which confer the right to occupy premises on payment of a regular sum (the rent) and subject to conditions. A tenancy may be granted for a fixed term, at the end of which it may be renewable by agreement with the landlord. Some tenancies are protected by law to prevent unlawful evictions. A tenant (residential or commercial) may, with the consent of the landlord, sub-let a room or the whole premises. Tenancy agreements often preclude sub-letting arrangements or require the landlord's written permission before sub-letting.

Under the Law of Property legislation, agreements involving land should be evidenced in writing. There are many forms of business lease or tenancy, but all should set out the respective rights and responsibilities of all parties. They usually have a good deal of 'small print' which may impose strict conditions regarding payment of rent and forfeiture if arrears of rent accrue, or financial liability for decoration, maintenance, payment of management fees, insurance for the building, and restrictions on type of use of the premises. It is vital to obtain a copy of the documents and check the relevant terms, ensuring that they are entirely compatible with the intended business use. Business tenancies and leases are regulated by complex legislation. To avoid the many potential legal pitfalls, anyone taking on any commercial (business) tenancy agreement or lease would be well advised to first seek legal advice from a conveyancing or commercial property lawyer or other expert. The voluntary *Code for Leasing Business Premises in England and Wales* (British Property Federation, 2007b) was the result of collaboration between commercial landlords and industry, representing owners (landlords) and occupiers (tenants). It is available for free download at www. leasingbusinesspremises.co.uk/.

A useful guide, *Renewing and Ending Business Leases: A Guide for Tenants and Landlords* (British Property Federation, 2004) is provided at the government website www.communities.gov.uk/publications/citiesandregions/renewingending.

Just a final note of caution. Property may be used for residential and/or for commercial purposes. On the sale of a lease, or on granting a lease, if a profit is made, there may be tax implications, e.g. capital gains tax.

8 Self-Employed Therapists

I like being self-employed, but hate doing accounts. Do I have to comply with some accounting rules for tax purposes?

When do I have to file my tax returns?

What if I am employed part of the week and work self-employed from home for the rest of the week?

How much do I have to earn before I am liable for VAT? Can I register voluntarily to save money?

If I fall ill, or die, who should I ask to contact clients to let them know and to cancel appointments? What about confidentiality here?

How should I store records at home?

Do I legally have to supply an 'out of hours' service to clients?

Are there rules about how and where I advertise and market myself as a counsellor or psychotherapist?

8.1 Setting up in business

8.1.1 Starting a business

It is quite possible to be employed part-time and also to run one's own self-employed business for the rest of the working week. Legally, this presents no undue difficulties, save that the therapist would be taxed under the PAYE system in respect of their employment and also have to register for self-employed taxation for the business (see Chapter 9 and 8.2 and 8.3 below). For help in making the distinction between self-employment and employment, see the HM Revenue and Customs Employment Status Indicator Tool at www.mrc.gov.uk/employment-status/index.htm. Section 8.3 gives further details of how to find out if you should be classified as 'self-employed' or not for tax purposes.

Therapy is regarded in law as a business within which a service is provided. New businesses can start at any time in the year, so a business tax year may run from the actual start date, or it can accord with the commonly used 'tax year' commencing on 6 April each year. For example, a business starting on 1 September might run its tax year from 1 September to 31 August the following year. For government advice and assistance on business start-up, see www.hmrc.gov.uk/

startingup/, and see tax returns at 8.3 below. There are a number of other possible sources of help for those starting in business. Local councils may encourage business groups and offer training or start-up loans, banks often have special offers, including business advice and free banking for the first year. There are useful information sheets on the BACP website, including: E1 Practical Aspects of *Setting up a Counselling Service* (Gabriel and Casemore 2008), G1 *Access to Records* (Bond and Jenkins, 2008), G2 *Breaches in Confidentiality* (Bond et al. 2009), G4 *Counselling and Psychotherapy Workloads* (Mearns 2004b), G5 *Personal Safety* (Jackson 2003), P1 *Professional Aspects of Setting up a Counselling Service* (Moore 2005), P2 *Charging for Therapy in Private Practice* (Dale 2008a), P6 *Introduction to Online Counselling and Psychotherapy* (Anthony 2007), and P11 *Making the Contract for Counselling and Psychotherapy* (Dale 2008a).

See also the perspectives of therapists themselves in the excellent edited book, *Freelance Counselling and Psychotherapy: Competition and Collaboration* (Clark 2002).

Checklist: Starting business

- Start date
- Set up premises where business operates (and/or services provided)
- Check that premises are covered by appropriate insurance
- Professional indemnity insurance for therapist(s)
- Professional memberships for therapist(s)
- Bank – advice and special offers for new businesses
- Local authority – training and networking opportunities
- Set up an administrative system for client records, appointments, standard letters, bills and receipts, invoices, etc.
- Computer data held? Data protection notification and registration
- Tax – registration as self-employed (if appropriate)
- VAT – registration (if appropriate)
- Services: business telephone/fax line
- Out-of-hours service arrangements (if appropriate)
- Local professional groups and organisations for marketing and support
- Advertising – local directory, *Yellow Pages* and websites.

8.1.2 Premises

Whether the business is run from home or from other premises does not matter for accounting purposes (see 8.2 below), but there are potential legal issues regarding the use of home or other premises for therapy, e.g. potential liability for capital gains tax (see Chapter 7). It is always best to take advice from an accountant or local business adviser.

8.1.3 Business equipment, amenities and resources

Business expenditure can be set against profits for tax purposes. Keep receipts for all equipment and bills used for the business. Sometimes only a proportion of the cost of equipment or expenditure can be allowed against income for taxation purposes (e.g. if a therapist uses the car for business, a proportion of the whole petrol cost may be allowable, or a proportion of heating costs if a therapist works from home). Ask the local tax office and/or see the websites listed below at 8.2, 8.3 and 8.4 for advice and help on taxation and VAT issues. If there is a dedicated telephone line or internet service used solely for the business, and the provider has a demarcation for business and residential users, consider whether the telephone or internet service should be registered for business use.

8.2 Accounting and book-keeping

All self-employed therapists must declare their income (business profits) for tax purposes, and HM Inland Revenue (HMIR) may ask for proof of the income and expenditure declared. The best way to provide proof acceptable to HMIR is to have good, clear business records of income and expenditure, created from and supported by all the relevant business documents, including invoices, cheque books, bank statements, paying-in books, and income and expenditure receipts. These records can be written up by the therapist personally (they do not necessarily have to be prepared or audited by an accountant or a book-keeper), but those of us who are not happy with figures may feel that the assistance of an accountant or book-keeper is well worth the cost. See www.hmrc.gov.uk/startingup/ for links to sources of advice and help.

Business bank accounts and income should be kept separate from personal accounts. Accounting books and separate sheets are available from stationers, and for computerised accounting Excel and other programmes provide spreadsheets, etc.

See 8.3 for tax returns. Data and supporting documents should be kept for seven years. Advice on business record keeping and resources can be found at www.hmrc.gov.uk/startingup/keeprecs.htm.

8.3 Self-employed tax returns and 'National Insurance' contributions

It is important to know whether you are self-employed or not. Local taxation offices will answer enquiries by telephone or personally, leaflet ES/FS1, which has useful government advice on how to make the decision, is available free from the local tax office or, with other informative leaflets, can be found at www.hmrc.gov.uk/employment-status/index.htm, see also Chapter 9 at 9.1.

The government website (www.hmrc.gov.uk/startingup/taxgate.htm) has a good deal of useful information about how National Insurance and taxation might affect the business, including the booklet SE1. *Thinking of Working for Yourself?* and leaflet IR56 *Employed or Self-Employed?* available at www.hmrc.gov.uk/pdfs/iv56.pdf.

8.4 VAT

VAT limits and the levels of VAT taxation are subject to government change, so will vary from year to year. Check on the government website below for up-to-date details. Currently, if, for example, your taxable turnover hits £68,000 a year (or you expect it to), you must register for VAT. You can register personally at a tax office or online. Details of the impact of VAT registration, how and where to register, and accounting schemes to simplify VAT accounting are all to be found at the government website www.hmrc.gov.uk/vat/start/register/index.htm. Check the website for updates on figures.

8.5 Insurance

Professional indemnity insurance (and public liability insurance, where appropriate, see Chapter 6) is, in our view, absolutely essential for the protection of clients and the therapist, no matter whether the therapist is self-employed or employed. Employer's liability insurance is required where therapists employ others. So too is appropriate insurance of the business premises since claims for injury against the occupier of premises can be expensive. Therapists working from home should always let their home and professional insurers know of their business use of the premises and ensure that their home insurance cover is not adversely affected by the business use. For more detailed discussion on this topic see Chapter 6.

8.6 Working from home

We discuss some of the issues about working from home in Chapter 7. Attention needs to be given not only to insurance (see 8.5 above and Chapter 6) and facilities in setting up the therapy room, but also to the impact on the client of coming to the therapist's home. For example, the inadvertent self-disclosures that we make just in the way that our home is decorated, furnished and organised, not to mention the possibility of unwanted intrusions from post, deliveries, family, pets and friends calling unexpectedly during sessions, or the risk of clients tripping over something left by the family in the hallway! For ideas and guidance, see all the BACP Information Sheets listed in 8.1 above.

8.7 Keeping and storing records, provision for illness and counselling 'wills'

One of the issues about working from home is the storage of client records and notes. For a full discussion of this see *Confidentiality and Record Keeping for Counsellors and Psychotherapists* (Bond and Mitchels 2008). We recommend keeping records safely and securely in a locked cabinet or other locked filing system, and ensuring adequate security of the premises as a whole with appropriate insurance cover for the premises and professional liability.

The issue then arises of who has the key to the cabinet and therefore access to client records? If we work from home, what would happen if we were to become ill or unable to work unexpectedly, and someone needed to let clients know and cancel appointments or make alternative therapy provision for them? Issues arise as to the confidentiality of client records in such a situation. We recommend that therapists make a 'counselling will', in which they make provisions for these eventualities and that therapists ensure that where confidentiality is a potential issue, clients are aware of and agree with the therapist's arrangements.

8.8 Out of hours arrangements

Some complaints and insurance claims arise because of difficulties or unexpected adverse events experienced by clients when making contact with therapists out of hours. Examples of these include family members answering the telephone or the front door; therapists not having time to deal with clients calling out of hours and giving the client insufficient empathic attention; voice, email or text messages left for the therapist not being treated as confidential, etc. Ensure that clients are aware of the therapist's boundaries and arrangements around out-of-hours contact, and negotiate these issues as part of the therapeutic contract where necessary. Protect the duty of confidentiality to clients by ensuring that if there is a business line at home, or a computer email program, family members do not answer that telephone and/or cannot access confidential therapy emails. If there is an answerphone, ensure that the content of any messages received on it is protected as confidential, and that messages are checked regularly.

8.9 Advertising, marketing and networking

Advertising must be accurate, open and honest, and comply with the Advertising Standards Authority (ASA) codes of practice. The latest, 11th edition of the *British Code of Advertising, Sales Promotion and Direct Marketing* which came into force in March 2003 is available free at www.asa.org.uk/asa/codes/. It is a criminal offence and also a ground for professional complaint and discipline to claim qualifications that you do not have, or services that you are not qualified to provide (see the Trade Descriptions Act 1968, the Business Protection from Misleading Marketing Regulations 2008 and the Consumer Protection from Unfair Trading Regulations 2008).

Local councils want to encourage the development of commerce locally, and so often provide training and opportunities for business networking. Entries in the telephone directory and in *Yellow Pages* can be helpful. *Yellow Pages* advertisements (see www.yell.com/) may carry a cost, so make sure that the address/telephone number cited are going to be effective in the long term. Private directories (e.g. www.thomson**local**.com/) also provide marketing opportunities. Many directories are also on the internet. Some internet directories (e.g. Google Local Business Centre, see www.google.com/**local**/add/, etc.) have automatic web links to internet maps showing the location of the business. This is great advertising, but first, consider whether you really want your home address (and a map of how to find it) available on the internet.

9 Therapist as Employer or Employee

The agency says that I am technically employed, even though I only work for them two days a week, and I'll have to go on their PAYE system. I believed that I was self-employed and could just invoice them. Who is right?

I work on Monday, Wednesday and Friday. As a part-time employee, I get two weeks holiday a year. When the agency is closed on public holidays, I can't work, but the Director says that the Bank Holiday Mondays are counted as part of my annual leave. That seems so unfair – what are my rights?

If our group of therapists employs a disabled receptionist part-time, do we have to make special arrangements for her?

A man at work keeps coming on to me. I have told him to keep away and tried to avoid him, but he is really persistent. What can I do?

I am the only woman in the agency, we all do the same job, but the men get paid more than me. I have said that I want the same pay, but nobody takes any notice.

I was warned verbally six weeks ago and have now received a written warning. If they sack me, what are my rights?

I have worked for the organisation for three years. Am I entitled to redundancy money if I have to go?

9.1 What is employment? Contracts of employment and contracts for services

The distinction between self-employment and employment is not always easy to make but it matters, because many of the statutory rights and duties described in this chapter (e.g. unfair dismissal and redundancy payments) apply only to employees. National Insurance Contributions and taxation systems differ too – employees pay Schedule E tax deducted under the PAYE system, and self-employed people pay Schedule D (see Chapter 8). For assistance in determination of status, see the helpful Inland Revenue guide at www.hmrc.gov.uk/page/employees/start-leave/status.htm and also the Employment status indicator at www.hmrc.gov.uk/calcs/esi.htm.

The employee/self-employed distinction largely depends on the nature of the contract between the parties, and the existence and definition of that contract. For contracts generally, see Chapter 4. In some situations there may be no contract, for example where an employment agency supplies temporary staff. The worker may have a contract with the agency and the agency may have a contract with the client organisation, but the worker may have no direct contract with the client organisation.

Services can be provided as an employee under a *contract of employment* (sometimes called a *contract of service*) or as a self-employed person under a *contract for services*. Employment (or not) is deduced from the contract and the surrounding circumstances.

Case law has established that contracts of employment must have certain characteristics:

1   The contract must impose an obligation on the employee to provide work personally.
2   There must be a continuity of work between employer and employee.
3   The worker must expressly or impliedly be subject to the control of the person for whom he works, sufficient to make that person master (i.e. the employee is under the employer's orders and directions).

Relevant circumstances defined by Cooke J in Market Investigations Ltd v Ministry of Social Security [1969] 2QB 173 were:

(a) He is employed as part of the business of the employer and his work is integral to that business
(b) He provides his own equipment
(c) He hires his own helpers
(d) He takes a degree of financial risk
(e) He has responsibility for investment and management and
(f) How far he has the opportunity of profiting from sound management in performing his task. (Cooke J at 185)

Additional factors may include:

•   Is person subject to internal grievance procedures?
•   Is there holiday pay, a pension scheme or other benefits such as health care?

Volunteers have been held not to be employees because they receive no payment for their work (see *Melhuish* v *Redbridge Citizens Advice Bureau* [2005] IRLR 419, EAT).

9.1.1 Can I have more than one employer?

Yes. A therapist might divide the working week between two employing organisations with two part-time jobs.

9.1.2 Can I have a different status at different times, e.g. be employed in one context and self-employed in another?

Yes. A therapist might, for example, work for one day each weekday as an unpaid volunteer for a charitable counselling organisation (not 'employed' at all); work three days for a salary on a contract of employment for another organisation (an employee); and also work from home as a self-employed therapist (self-employed).

9.2 Employer responsibilities

9.2.1 Health and safety in the workplace

The employer is under a duty to comply with the health and safety legislation and to provide a safe workplace for their workforce (see Chapter 7 at 7.2 for discussion of the health and safety legislation, and 7.3 for public liability insurance).

9.2.2 Insurance

Employers have a duty to provide insurance for their workers and to display (physically or electronically) a certificate for inspection (see Chapter 6 at 6.9 for employer's liability insurance).

9.3 Holidays ('annual leave' and 'additional leave')

The Working Time Regulations 1998, as amended by the Working Time (Amendment) Regulations 2001, establish a worker's right to paid annual leave which is not subject to a requirement of prior continuous service. Annual leave entitlements are based on the 'leave year', commencing on the date in the 'relevant agreement', which is a collective workforce agreement usually incorporated into the contract of employment.

Each worker is entitled to four weeks annual leave in each leave year, calculated as 20 leave days each year for a person working a five day week. In the regulations, public holidays (eight days in the UK) count towards the leave entitlement. This led to Trade Union protests, and from leave years commencing on 1 April 2009, employers are now required to give 'additional leave', totalling 5.6 weeks (28 days). However, this is a maximum, so does not benefit those who work more than a five-day week. However, employers can of course be generous and give more annual leave than the minimum entitlement.

For health and safety reasons, annual leave cannot be carried over from one year to the next, nor can a worker be paid in lieu of taking leave, unless at the end of his employment. Additional leave is treated differently. It can be carried over, but only into the following leave year (and not subsequent leave years). There is no payment in lieu of taking additional leave.

Part-time workers should expect their leave entitlement to be worked out on a pro rata basis according to the number of days they work.

In the first year of work, leave accrues at the rate of 1/12 of the entitlement on the first day of each month, and (unless otherwise agreed with the employer) workers can take leave only after it has accrued. For all subsequent years of work, leave can be taken at any time in the leave year.

9.4 Maternity, parental rights and paternity leave

9.4.1 Maternity leave and parental rights

Most of the law relating to maternity leave and pay can be found in the Employment Relations Act 1999 (ERA 1999), the Maternity and Parental Leave, etc. Regulations 1999, and the Employment Act 2002 (EA 2002).

Subject to the appropriate qualifying conditions (see Slade 2008: 33), female employees are entitled to:

- paid time off for ante-natal care
- 26 weeks ordinary maternity leave and 26 weeks additional maternity leave
- protection from dismissal or detriment by reason of pregnancy or childbirth
- maternity pay
- the right to return to work after maternity leave
- an offer of alternative work before suspension on maternity grounds and remuneration on suspension on maternity grounds.

Parental leave of 13 weeks for each child, or 18 weeks for a disabled child, is exercisable by any employee (with one year's continuous service) who has, or expects to have, parental responsibility for a child. This is available in blocks of a week at a time.

9.4.2 Paternity leave

The Employment Act 2002 and the Paternity and Adoption Leave Regulations 2002 created the right of unpaid paternity leave of one week, or two consecutive weeks, for a father of a child who has been employed continuously for 26 weeks (ending with the 14th week before the due date of birth). There is similar protection against dismissal or detriment etc., as described above for maternity leave. Adoption leave can be for a period of 26 weeks, in the same way as maternity leave.

9.5 Termination of employment and rights on leaving work

Employment may be ended in a number of ways, including mutual agreement, expiry of the contract, frustration (where, through no fault of employer or employee, it becomes impossible for the contract to continue) or notice given by the employee. It may also end through a fundamental breach of the contract (by employer or employee) or dismissal, and these may lead to a claim for unfair dismissal, wrongful dismissal or redundancy.

On leaving employment, the worker is entitled to:

- notice in accordance with statute – if employed between one month and two years, notice is one week; if employed between two and12 years, one week for each year employed; and after 12 years for a maximum of 12 weeks
- payment for any leave accrued but not yet taken
- payment in lieu of notice
- written statement of reasons for dismissal (if dismissed).

9.6 Discrimination and equal opportunities in the workplace

Unlawful discrimination in the workplace includes:

- **Disability discrimination** (see 9.6.1 below)
- **Discrimination on the grounds of sex, sexual orientation or gender reassignment** (see the Sex Discrimination Act 1975, the Equal Treatment Directive (76/207/EEC) and the Equal Opportunities Directive (2006/54/EC) implementing equal opportunities, e.g. equal pay. See also the provisions relating to sexual orientation and sexual discrimination in the Employment Equality (Sex Discrimination) Regulations 2005, Employment Equality (Sexual Orientation) Regulations 2003 and the Employment Equality (Sexual Orientation) Regulations 2003 (Amendment) Regulations 2004
- **Age discrimination (**see the Employment Equality (Age) Regulations 2006, which have been in force since 1 October 2006)
- **Discrimination on the grounds of religion or belief (**see the Employment Equality (Religion or Belief) Regulations 2003)
- **Discrimination on the grounds of race** (see the Race Relations Act 1976).

In addition, it is unlawful to discriminate on the grounds of:

- pregnancy, maternity leave or paternity leave (see 9.4 above)
- marital or civil partnership status (see the Sex Discrimination Act 1975, as amended by the Civil Partnership Act 2004, s. 251 (1)–(2).

Part-time workers are protected in relation to pay and other potential detriments by the Part-time Workers (Prevention of Less Favourable Treatment) Regulations 2000.

9.6.1 Disability discrimination

For a definition of disability and discussion of the general application of the Disability Discrimination Acts 1995 and 2005, with resources for information and help, see Chapter 7 at 7.1 and the website www.direct.gov.uk/en/DisabledPeople RightsAndObligations/DisabilityRights/DG_4001068. Braille, Audio, BSL and Easy read versions are available from The Stationery Office at www. tsoshop.co.uk. In the context of employment, see the *Disability Discrimination Act 1995 Code of Practice: Employment and Occupation* (the *Code*), issued on 1 October 2004, setting out the rights of disabled workers and duties of their employers.

The *Code* provides that employers should not discriminate against disabled workers, but this is now limited by the House of Lords' decision in *London Borough of Lewisham* v *Malcolm* [2008] UKHL 43, overruling earlier decisions, which may influence future employment cases. It is now not enough for a disabled person to show that there was some connection between her disability and the reason for the treatment that she challenges. She also needs to show that her disability played some motivating part in the alleged discrimination.

See Table 9.1 for forms of disability discrimination, and Table 9.2 for examples of reasonable adjustments that, in the event of a claim of discrimination made under the DDA 1995, employers might (or might not) be expected to make.

Table 9.1   Forms of discrimination

The information about forms of discrimination in this table is derived from the *Disability Discrimination Act 1995 Code of Practice: Employment and Occupation*, issued on 1 October 2004.

Indirect discrimination
No clear legislation, but general duty to make 'reasonable adjustments' wherever a provision, criterion or practice places a disabled person at a substantial disadvantage as compared to a non-disabled person.

A case concerning a claim made under the DDA 1995 by the carer of a disabled person on the grounds of 'associative discrimination' is currently under consideration in the European Court of Justice (see *Attridge Law* v *Coleman* [2007] ICR 654, [2007] IRLR 88). The Advocate General's opinion, delivered on 31 January 2008, supports the view that a person who is not disabled may make such a claim.

Direct discrimination
Occurs in relation to an employer where, 'on the ground of the disabled person's disability, he treats the disabled person less favourably than he treats or would treat a person not having that particular disability, whose relevant circumstances, including his abilities, are the same as, or not materially different from, those of the disabled person' (Slade 2008: 151). The offence needs a comparator, and the defence of justification does not apply in offences under DDA 1995, s. 3 (A)(4) and s. 3(A)(5).

Disability-related discrimination
The term 'disability-related discrimination' is not in the DDA 1995. It is a convenient shorthand used in the *Code* to describe the type of discrimination that before 1 October 2004 was referred to as 'direct discrimination'.

Examples of direct discrimination and disability-related discrimination

Situation of disabled person	Comparator	Is this direct discrimination?	Law and guidance
Typist can do 30 wpm is refused a job, and job is offered to a non-disabled person	Non-disabled typist who can do 30 wpm (i.e. circumstances are the same or not materially different, e.g. here it is ability)	Yes	*Code*, paras 4.2.0– 4.2.1

Table 9.1 *(Continued)*

Situation of disabled person	Is there justification for the actions complained of?	Is this disability-related? discrimination	Law and guidance
Blind employee not offered job on assumption that she was unable to use a computer	General assumptions unlikely to be justifiable	Yes	*Code*, paras 6.3–6.7
Employee using wheelchair is not promoted solely because work station for senior post has no wheelchair access	Refusal to promote would not be justified if adjustment is possible (i.e. furniture could be rearranged to provide wheelchair access)	Yes	DDA 1995, s. 3(A)(6)

Table 9.2 Reasonable adjustments that employers might make for disabled employees

Employers are not specifically required to make reasonable adjustments for disabled employees, but the responsibility is implied, in that if a claim of discrimination is brought by an employee, then what would be a reasonable adjustment is assessed. This is defined in the context of the Disability Discrimination Act 1995 (DDA 1995), s 18(B), and the Disability Discrimination Act 1995 *Code of Practice: Employment and Occupation* (the *Code*), issued on 1 October 2004. Other adjustments listed here have been held by the Employment Tribunal to be reasonable.

In determining reasonableness, regard should be given to practicality, the employer's finances, costs, disruption to the work and to others, the general size of the business undertaking, and the co-operation of the employee. A small organisation or a therapist working from home would not be expected to do as much as a large employer.

Nature of adjustment	Law and guidance
Widening doorway or moving light switches	DDA 1995 and the *Code*, para 5.18
Allocation of some duties to another person	DDA 1995 and the *Code*, para 5.18
Transfer disabled person to fill existing vacancy	DDA 1995 and the *Code*, para 5.18
Alter working hours	DDA 1995 and the *Code*, para 5.18
Assign disabled person to another place of work	DDA 1995 and the *Code*, para 5.18
Allow employee to be absent during working hours (e.g. for rehabilitation, assessment, treatment, etc.)	DDA 1995 and the *Code*, para 5.18

(Continued)

Table 9.2   *(Continued)*

Nature of adjustment	Law and guidance
Provision of training or mentoring	DDA 1995 and the *Code*, para 5.18
Acquiring or modifying equipment (e.g. adapting computers, headphones etc.)	DDA 1995 and the *Code*, para 5.18
Modifying instructions or reference manuals	DDA 1995 and the *Code*, para 5.18
Modifying procedures for testing or assessment	DDA 1995 and the *Code*, para 5.18
Providing a reader or interpreter	DDA 1995 and the *Code*, para 5.18
Providing supervision (e.g. where disability has led to lack of confidence)	DDA 1995 and the *Code*, para 5.18
Provision of subtitled training videos	Employment Tribunal Decision
Discounting disability-related absences in assessing absence record	Employment Tribunal Decision
Adjustments it is not reasonable to expect an employer to provide	**Law and guidance**
Transport to and from work	DDA 1995, s. 4 (A)
Personal carer to assist with toilet needs (as not job related)	*Kenny* v *Hampshire Constabulary* [1999] IRLR 76
Adjustments where the employer did not know and/or could not reasonably be expected to know of the employees disability	DDA 1995, s. 4(A)(3)(b)

9.6.2 Equal pay

The main body of law is in the Equal Pay Act 1970, as amended by many subsequent pieces of legislation. In addition to the rules prohibiting discrimination described in 9.6 above, the legislation provides in various ways that women employed in an establishment in Great Britain (whether they are British or not) should receive 'equal pay for equal work' in comparison with men. The provisions for equal treatment apply both to men and women (see s. 1(13)).

The way the law operates is that clauses in contracts of employment which are less favourable are modified by the legislation to make the employee entitled to equal terms. For example, if a man and a woman do the same job, but he is paid £500 and she gets £350, she is entitled to £500, or if she has a clause giving her some extra benefit that he does not have, he would be entitled to that benefit too (except that maternity and paternity leave are different – see 9.4 above).

Part-time workers are protected in relation to pay by the Part-time Workers (Prevention of Less Favourable Treatment) Regulations 2000. See also the Equal Opportunities Commissions Code of Practice on Equal Pay (2003).

'Equality' in relation to work is interpreted as meaning:

- like work
- work rated as an equivalent
- work of like value.

9.7 Harassment

The Protection from Harassment Act 1997 was designed to protect victims of harassment, whatever form the harassment takes, wherever it occurs, and whatever its motivation. Harassment is unlawful and may occur in the context of any of the forms of discrimination listed in 9.6 above. In the workplace, harassment may involve the violation of dignity or the creation of a hostile working environment.

Harassment can take various forms, depending on the context in which it happens. Breaches of the Protection from Harassment Act 1997 may constitute a criminal offence, or may give rise to civil liability, or both. The Act (as amended by subsequent legislation), with specified exceptions, states in s. 1:

(1) A person may not pursue a course of conduct

(a) which amounts to harassment of another and
(b) which he knows or ought to know amounts to harassment of the other.

A 'course of conduct' implies an action on at least two occasions, s. 7(2)(3) and 'conduct' includes speech, s. 7 (1)(2). If the actions are separated by several months with no causal link between them, the court finding a 'course of conduct' is less likely than when actions are close together, e.g. within three months of each other (see *Pratt* v DPP [2001] EWHC 483). The test applied by the courts as to whether the potential offender 'ought to know' that the actions amounted to harassment is what a reasonable person with the same information might think in a similar situation. Clearly, physical violence or threats of violence are likely to constitute criminal harassment, and repeated verbal aggression may also constitute harassment.

Section 2 creates the criminal offence of pursuit of a course of conduct in breach of s. 1. Criminal proceedings can deal only with offences which have been committed. Section 3 goes further. It affords victims a civil remedy in respect both of actual breaches of s. 1 and also threatened breaches. For instance, a single act of harassment may have occurred, which is not in itself a course of conduct, and the victim may fear repetition. Section 3 provides:

(1) An actual or apprehended breach of section 1 may be the subject of a claim in civil proceedings by the person who is or may be the victim of the course of conduct in question.

(2) On such a claim damages may be awarded for (among other things) any anxiety caused by the harassment and any financial loss resulting from the harassment.

Subsequent provisions in the section make plain that the court may grant an injunction for the purpose of restraining a defendant from pursuing any conduct which amounts to harassment. Breach, without reasonable excuse, of such an injunction is itself a criminal offence (see subsection (6))

It follows that in the workplace, harassment might take the form of a criminal offence if the actions taken amounted to a sufficient level, causing the victim 'alarm' or 'distress' (s. 7 (2)). Three threatening or abusive phone calls may constitute harassment, as in the case of *Kelly* v DPP [2002] EWHC Admin 1428 166 JP 621.

It is our view that threatening email and internet communications may also constitute harassment if they cause alarm and distress to the recipient (see *S* v *DPP* [2008] EWHC (Admin) 438).

An interesting and leading case on this topic is the House of Lords decision in *Majrowski* v *Guy's and St Thomas's NHS Trust* [2006] UKHL 34. In this case, an employee, a clinical auditor, was subjected to criticism and bullying by his departmental manager, who was rude, abusive and critical to him in front of other staff, imposing unrealistic targets and threatening disciplinary action if these were not met. Their Lordships' opinions in this leading case about employer's liability for the actions of employees are also reported online at www.publications.parliament. uk/pa/ld200506/ldjudgmt/jd060712/majro-1.htm. In this case, the court supported the concept of the 'vicarious liability' of employers for acts of their employees in the course of their employment, and reiterated that imposing this strict liability on employers encourages them to maintain standards of good practice by their employees. For those reasons, where one employee harasses another, the employer may be held liable. Employers can cover their potential liability with appropriate insurance and prices. For a detailed discussion of the relevant law, see the judgment in the *Majrowski* case and Slade (2008: chapter 12).

The criminal offence of harassment is punishable with a fine or imprisonment (s. 2), and also may be the subject of a civil claim in the High Court or the county court, attracting a variety of civil penalties, such as an injunction (court order to desist from an action), damages and/or financial compensation for anxiety caused or for financial loss (s. 3). Breach of a civil injunction can be punished by a fine for contempt of court or may become a criminal offence, followed by a warrant for arrest and criminal penalties.

A final point should be noted on the interpretation of the Protection from Harassment Act 1997. Sections 1–7 of that Act apply to England and Wales. Sections 8–11 make corresponding provision for Scotland. Section 10 inserts a new section, s. 18B, into the Prescription and Limitation (Scotland) Act 1973. The new s. 18B envisages that the employer of a person responsible for harassment may be the defender in an action of harassment. In other words, s. 18B appears to assume that in Scotland an employer may be vicariously liable.

9.8 Disciplinary issues, warnings and sacking

The Employment Act 2008 (EA 2008) received royal assent on 13 November 2008, and when in force, it will be effective in England, Scotland and Wales. Parts of it (ss. 8–14) will affect legislation concerning the National Minimum Wage in Northern Ireland. It replaces part of the earlier Employment Act 2002. Together, these Acts set out a *Code of Practice* for discipline and resolving grievances to be followed before dismissal. The legislation is not yet compulsory for all employment contracts.

For an explanation of current employment rights, see the various headings in the government website www.direct.gov.uk/en/Employment/index.htm. To download all the legislation and guidance as documents from the internet, see www.berr.gov.uk/whatwedo/employment/employment-legislation/employment-act-2008/index.html. To read the guidance to the EA 2008, go to www.opsi.gov.uk/acts/acts2008/en/ukpgaen_20080024_en_1.htm.

9.9 Employment Tribunal

The Employment Tribunal was a body set up by The Employment Tribunals Act 1996. With powers under that Act, and also the Tribunals, Courts and Enforcement Act 2007, it determines cases of alleged 'unfair dismissal' and other employment matters, with the power to award various remedies, including reinstatement, re-engagement, compensation and costs, to employees where the employer has failed to comply with the relevant *Code of Practice*. Although the Employment Tribunal already has power to determine an application without a hearing, this has not so far been used, but will now be encouraged under the EA 2008. Hearings can be postponed for a fixed period while attempts are made at conciliation with ACAS or other conciliation services.

9.10 Retirements and pensions

Under current UK law, an employee reaches the 'retirement age' at 65. Women born during or before 1949 may choose to retire at the age of 60. Women born between 1949 and 1956 will have a gradually increasing retirement age up to 65. At that age retirement benefits (retirement pension) are payable, and National Insurance Contributions are no longer required. National retirement pensions may be postponed upon request. For details of money, tax and retirement benefits (pensions) see www.direct.gov.uk.

It is unlawful to discriminate against employees on the grounds of age (see the Employment Equality (Age) Regulations 2006). Nevertheless, in the UK employers can dismiss employees over the age of 65 without redundancy payments. In 2009, Heyday (part of Age Concern) challenged employers' right to force retirement, bringing a case before the European Court of Justice (ECJ) on the basis that it breached equality regulations. However, the ECJ held that it is permissible as long as it is part of a social policy objective and not just to cut costs.

9.11 Redundancy

Redundancy is a form of dismissal from employment not as a result of the employee's fault, but usually because the workforce is being changed or reduced or the employee's services are no longer required for some other reason. There are rights with redundancy, depending on the nature of the employment contract, length of service, etc. For guidance on redundancy rights, see the leaflets produced by the Department of Trade and Industry: *Redundancy Payments* (URN 98/95), *Offsetting Pensions Against Redundancy Payments* (RLP1), and *Time Off for Job Hunting when Facing Redundancy* (PL703). See also the website www.direct.gov. uk/en/Employment/RedundancyAndLeavingYourJob/Redundancy/DG_10026616.

9.12 Criminal records and disclosures

In Chapter 5 at 5.11, we considered the new safeguarding procedures for children and vulnerable adults. We mentioned briefly in 5.10 the current role of the Criminal Records Bureau, but the changing role of criminal records checks in the context of the new safeguarding procedures in the UK will gradually become clearer as the new legislation and procedures are implemented over the next few years. Watch for news of developments on the website for the Independent Safeguarding Authority (ISA) at www.isa.gov.uk.

Details of the procedure regarding disclosure of criminal records is available from the Criminal Records Bureau (CRB) at their website www.crb.gov.uk. In Scotland, records are kept by the CRBS and applications made to Disclosure Scotland (www.disclosureScotland.co.uk/) apply. In Northern Ireland, apply to Access Northern Ireland at www.accessni.gov.uk. For the current provisions see also Monitoring Procedures and Safeguards in Chapter 5 at 5.11.

There are two types of 'CRB check', described as 'standard' and 'enhanced'.

Alongside the provisions of the safeguarding Vulnerable Groups Act 2006 and the Protection of Vulnerable Groups (Scotland) Act 2007 (PVGA 2007) described in Chapter 5, a standard or enhanced criminal records check may continue to be a job requirement for those who work with children or vulnerable people, whether in paid employment or as volunteers. Self-employed people may need to use an umbrella organisation for their criminal records check.

Under the Police Act 1997, access may be requested by employers and registered bodies for the records of a person's past convictions, but it does not indicate whether an applicant is permitted to work within the UK. The employer has liability for ensuring that the person they intend to employ does not have any restriction on their ability to take up employment within the UK. For further information on the rules surrounding working in the UK go to the Borders and Immigration Agency website at www.ind.homeoffice.gov.uk/workingintheuk.

Until voluntary ISA registration is available (see Chapter 5 at 5.11), and for certain people to whom ISA registration (or the PVGA 2007 provisions in Scotland) does not apply, criminal records checks will continue to be necessary for some posts involving contact with children or vulnerable adults. In general, the type of work will involve some aspect of caring for, supervising, training or being in sole charge of such people. This group could include teachers, youth workers, care staff and therapists working with children and vulnerable adults. Enhanced checks are also issued for certain statutory purposes such as gaming and lottery licences. See also the Police Act 1997 (Criminal Records) (Registration) Regulations 2006 and the Police Act 1997 (Criminal Records) (Registration) (Scotland) Regulations 2006.

On payment of a fee, an applicant may request either a Standard CRB check or an enhanced CRB check.

Standard CRB Check:

This provides the following information:

- convictions, cautions, reprimands and warnings held on the Police National Computer in England and Wales, and most of the relevant convictions in Scotland and Northern Ireland may be included
- Information held by local police forces relating to relevant non-conviction information
- Information from the Government's Child First list (formerly PoCA, see Chapter 5)
- Information from the Government's Adults First List (formerly PoVA, see Chapter 5)
- Information held by the Department for Children, Schools and Families (DCSF) under s. 142 Education Act 1949 (formerly List 99).

A 'criminal conviction certificate' is 'basic disclosure', as defined by the Criminal Records Bureau Revised Code of Practice (CRB 2009). It lists all current convictions (but excluding those affected by the Rehabilitation of Offenders Act 1974), or confirms that there are no convictions. This is not yet in force in England and Wales, but is available in Scotland from Disclosure Scotland.

Enhanced CRB Check:

Enhanced checks contain the same information as standard checks but with the addition of any locally held police force information considered relevant to the job role.

10 Dealing with Legal Claims and Going to Court

I don't understand the difference between criminal and civil trials. The law all seems so foreign to me.

I am only owed a small amount, but is it worth taking to court?

How do I make a civil claim for a debt? I have no idea where to go or what to do!

What if I don't agree with the order made by the court?

Do I have to produce my notes when a solicitor writes and asks for them?

My client is a witness for the prosecution in a criminal trial next month. The defence have warned me that they might want me to go to court. They know about her past, and I think they want to use me to discredit my client. Can I refuse to go?

I have been asked to do anger and stress management work with a mother whose child is subject to care proceedings. Where can I get information and advice about what the court (and social services) might expect of me?

The family are arguing over contact. Their case is now in the county court and the solicitor for the children's mother has asked to talk with me over the phone. She also said that she wants me to go and give evidence about the father's alcohol dependency. Do I have to do as she asks?

What do I call the judge?

Can I sit down when I give evidence?

In Chapter 1, we looked at the structure of the UK legal system and the civil and criminal courts in the three jurisdictions of England and Wales, Scotland and Northern Ireland. The law in this chapter relates solely to England and Wales, with specific examples from the other jurisdictions where appropriate.

In Chapter 1 we explored the interface between civil and criminal law, seeing how the same action might constitute both a civil wrong and also potentially a crime. For example, a male therapist who makes unwanted sexual advances to a young client is likely to be:

- failing to comply with ethical standards of practice (therefore a complaint may lead to disciplinary proceedings)

- in breach of the duty of care to the client (a breach of the therapeutic contract also potentially leading to a claim for negligence)
- and possibly also committing the criminal offence of sexual assault.

Chapter 1 explained the legal system and the roles of the different courts. This chapter explores the ways in which the therapist may make or respond to claims in the course of work, focusing on the county court. It then briefly explores the therapist's professional role in other courts and cases.

Her Majesty's Courts Service (HMCS) is responsible for managing the courts system in England and Wales, and the website www.hmcourts-service.gov.uk/ has a wealth of information about the courts and proceedings, with a series of leaflets and forms which guide readers through each court process. All the leaflets and forms mentioned below are available from that website, or from the courts, free of charge. No website, leaflet or book is a substitute for good legal advice based on the facts of each particular case, so consult a lawyer or other professional wherever necessary. Professional indemnity insurance often includes free legal advice. More useful resources are listed in the back of the book.

10.1 Making and responding to civil claims in the county court

HMCS provide a series of useful guidance leaflets, all of which are available free from their website or from the local court office. Before starting to make a claim, see *Making a Claim? Some Questions to Ask Yourself* (HMCS, Leaflet EX301).

10.1.1 What can I claim for in the county court?

The county court deals with a wide variety of cases, including divorce, dissolution of civil partnerships, adoption, wills and probate, personal injury (e.g. accident claims), family matters (e.g. disputes about contact with a child and an absent parent), and property matters. Therapists might become involved in any of these types of case, but in the course of their work, are most likely to make claims for unpaid debts and other contract and consumer claims (see Chapter 4 for discussion, e.g. failure to pay for goods sold, faulty goods or workmanship), disputes about ownership of goods, or disputes between landlords and tenants about repairs, deposits or rent arrears.

A claim may be made in the county court for a set sum (e.g. £750 for unpaid fees), or for a sum to be determined by the court (e.g. such sum as the court thinks fit to compensate for loss of three weeks work through closure of premises).

We will concentrate here on contract and consumer claims, in which the county court can give a variety of remedies, for example damages (a sum of money), injunctions (orders not to do something), mandates (orders to do something such as restitution) and costs. In some cases, it may also issue warnings and warrants for arrest for breach of orders.

10.1.2 How do I make a claim?

The procedure for making a claim is explained in *How to Make a Claim* (HMCS, Leaflet EX302). See also *Debt Recovery for Businesses* (Leaflet EX350). The court will expect that before a claim is made in the county court, an attempt will have been made to resolve the matter by correspondence, and failing that, by mediation or arbitration schemes. It is only when these fail that court action is appropriate.

A claim is made by completion of the necessary forms and payment of a fee to the court, calculated on the amount claimed. The forms are available from the court or the website (www.hmcourts-service.gov.uk). Court fees vary and are subject to government changes. Also, some people are exempt (see Leaflet EX60A *Court Fees – Do I Have to Pay Them?*). It is best to check with the court in each case.

Once a claim is made, the defendant should reply and either admit or dispute all or part of the claim. If no reply is received, then see Leaflet EX304, *No Reply to My Claim Form – What Should I Do?* If the defendant replies and disputes the claim, see *The Defendant Disputes All or Part of My Claim* (Leaflet EX306). If all or part of the claim is admitted, see *The Defendant Admits My Claim – I Claimed a Fixed Amount of Money* (Leaflet EX309) or *The Defendant Admits My Claim – I Did Not Claim a Fixed Amount of Money* (Leaflet EX308).

Once the position is clear, then the claim may be listed by the court for hearing in two ways: *The Small Claims Track* (Leaflet EX307) (see 10.3 below) or *The Fast Track and the Multi Track* (Leaflet EX305).

10.1.3 Making a claim in Scotland

In Scotland, civil claims can be raised in the Sheriff Court or the Court of Session. Sheriff Courts are situated throughout Scotland. It is usually less expensive to raise proceedings in the Sheriff Court, and therefore in a relatively low value case the best course of action would be to litigate in the Sheriff Courts. There are three different types of procedure available, depending on the sum which you want to sue for. Small Claims cases are for the lowest value claims and have an upper limit of £3,000. Cases worth between £3,000 and £5,000 follow the Summary Cause procedure. Cases worth anything over £5,000 follow the Ordinary Cause procedure. You can represent yourself at the Sheriff Court if you wish, although it is generally better to have a solicitor acting on your behalf. Further information, including the forms you have to complete to raise a claim, can be found at www.scotcourts. gov.uk. The Court of Session deals with higher value and more complex cases. If you are in doubt, a solicitor will be able to advise you on the best court in which to raise an action.

10.1.4 Defending a claim in the county court

When a claim is made, the defendant should reply and either admit or dispute all or part of the claim. Leaflet EX303, *A Claim Has Been Made Against Me – What Should I Do?*, explains how to respond to notification of a claim. Some claims may be defended with the court's 'Money Claim On Line' at www.hmcourts-service.gov. uk/onlineservices/mcol/index.htm (see below at 10.2).

10.1.5 Defending a claim in Scotland

If you receive service of a summons or initial writ where the proceedings have been raised in a Scottish court, then the procedure you will need to follow will depend on the type of claim raised against you. You should contact a solicitor, or the court where the case has been raised immediately to find out what you need to do to protect your position. If you (or a solicitor acting on your behalf) don't indicate your intention to defend the proceedings to the court, then 'decree' can pass against you. This means that the person who raised the claim against you will have a court order against you which they can seek to have enforced in various ways (including by seizing property or money in a bank account). Decree passing against you is likely to significantly affect your credit rating and should be avoided at all costs. If decree passes, you can seek to have it recalled in certain circumstances.

10.2 'Money Claim On Line' procedure

The courts are trying to make life easier by using internet technology to make and defend claims in the county court. Although online, the same court principles and rules will apply. Claims (currently those below £99,999.99 and against no more than two defendants) may be made and defended using 'Money Claim On Line' at www.hmcourts-service.gov.uk/onlineservices/mcol/index.htm. To start this claim procedure, simply log in and click on the link, following the online instructions. See the Civil Procedure Rules 1998, as amended. The updates to these rules are listed in the references.

There is no online claims procedure in Scotland.

10.3 County court 'small claims procedure' and the 'fast track' procedure

See the government website at www.direct.gov.uk. The county court has a special procedure for dealing with 'small claims' where the parties can conduct the proceedings themselves. For information and guidance, see www.hmcourts-service.gov.uk/infoabout/claims/index.htm, from which forms and guidance can be viewed and downloaded. Currently, 'small claims' are defined as cases where the amount in dispute is under £5,000, and the case does not involve complex law, evidence or procedure. The main types of small claim which therapists might encounter are unpaid debts, and we have used this here as an illustrative example.

If a therapist is owed money, a claim may be made for a set sum, e.g. £450 for unpaid fees. The small claims procedure is appropriate. A court fee is payable, calculated on the amount of the claim made. Fees vary, and can be changed from time to time by the government, so check with the court in each case.

Once the sum claimed and the legal position is clear, then the claim may be listed by the court for hearing in one of three ways:

- *The Small Claims Track* may be appropriate for values under £5,000 (Leaflet EX307).
- *The Fast Track* procedure is for claims over £5,000, which are considered more suitable for the main county court. The court may then send out Leaflet EX305, *The Fast Track and the Multi Track*. For claims issued after 6 April 2009, the financial limit of the fast track procedure was increased to £25,000. Costs in fast track cases are also limited to specified sums.
- A multi-track claim is for complex cases involving sums exceeding £25,000.

The judge deciding a small claims track case may offer the parties the opportunity to be heard, or may feel that the case can be decided without a court hearing. Small claims mediation may be offered to settle the claim. Parties will be notified of this and given a chance to make representations if they wish.

There are useful leaflets about attending the county court, EX341 – *I Have Been Asked to be a Witness – What Do I Do? – and EX342 – Some Things You Should Know about Coming to a Court Hearing*.

10.4 High Court

The High Court has several divisions, each of which deals with different areas of work and the more serious cases, including appeals (see Chapter 1). High Court procedure is therefore both more complex and expensive than the county court. We firmly recommend seeking legal advice and assistance before commencing proceedings in the High Court. For guidance on giving evidence in court see 10.9 below.

10.5 Criminal cases

Criminal cases are tried in the magistrates' court or the Crown Court, depending on the type of case and its severity, and in some cases the prosecution and defence may make representations to the court about where the case should be heard. Cases may begin in the magistrates' court and be committed to the Crown Court for trial. The criminal prosecution and appeals system is briefly explained in Chapter 1.

Therapists may be asked to give evidence in criminal cases by the prosecution or by the defence. Usually a request comes via the police or Crown Prosecution Service or from a defendant acting in person or the solicitors acting for the defendant. If a request for notes comes, see 10.8 below and refer to Bond and Sandhu (2005) for a full discussion of responding to a request to give evidence in a criminal court. For general guidance on being a witness in any court, see 10.9 below. Therapy with children or adults who may be witness in court proceedings is subject to certain controls. See the *Memorandum of Good Practice in Video Recorded Interviews with Child Witnesses in Criminal Proceedings* (Home Office 1996) and also

Crown Prosecution Service (England and Wales) (2005), *The CPS: Provision of Therapy for Vulnerable or Intimidated Adult Witnesses Prior to a Criminal Trial – Practice Guidance*, which is also available at www.cps.gov.uk.

In Scotland, therapists may be cited as witnesses to attend at the district court, Sheriff Court or Court of Session. Information for people cited as witnesses in criminal proceedings in Scotland is available at www.scotcourts.gov.uk/courtusers/witnesses/index.asp.

10.6 Child protection cases

Therapists working with children and families may become involved from time to time in child protection cases, where the state intervenes in family life to protect a child from present or future harm. The various government agencies, e.g. local authorities, NHS, education and police, are expected to co-operate to protect children. Sadly, the system sometimes fails, resulting in continuing abuse and the tragic death of children such as Victoria Climbié in 2000, which led to the *Every Child Matters* reforms (DfES 2004a and b) and the Children Act 2004.

We discussed the role of therapists in child protection in *Confidentiality and Record Keeping* (Bond and Mitchels 2008: 35, 38–9 and 96–9).

> Teachers, doctors and other professionals, including counsellors, may be the first recipients of a child's disclosure of abuse or neglect. Victoria Climbié never got as far as seeing a counsellor. It is salutary to ask ourselves how we as therapists would respond in a similar situation in judging the balance between respecting privacy and confidentiality and the dangers to the child concerned or the balance between the rights of adult 'carers' and the child. Children's services are currently being restructured as a result of the Laming Report (Laming 2003). As a consequence, more therapists may become involved in working for the new services or alongside them.
>
> (Bond and Mitchels 2008: 40)

Recommendations for reform are often triggered by another tragic failure of the system, for example the death of Baby P and the recent report of Lord Laming (2009). There are always new developments in child protection practice, some of which may involve therapists in undertaking assessments or therapeutic work with children and families and/or to provide evidence in matters concerning children. All therapists should familiarise themselves with the current government guidance, *What To Do If You are Worried that a Child is Being Abused* (DfES 2006a). Those working within the NHS should also refer to *Confidentiality: NHS Code of Practice* (DH 2003). The current child protection procedures and the role of professionals are set out in detail in *Working Together to Safeguard Children* (DfES 2006c). See also the *Framework for Assessment of Children in Need and their Families* (DH 2000), but watch for changes. For a child's right to confidentiality and capacity to consent to assessments and disclosure of information see Chapter 11 (Bond and Mitchels 2008: Chapter 11). For Scotland, see the Scottish Executive guidance (Scottish Executive 2003; 2004a and b; The Scottish Office 1998a and b).

10.7 Private family cases

The Family Court has three tiers, the magistrates' court, county court and High Court levels, and cases can move freely up and down these tiers, as explained in Chapter 1. Family cases concerning adoption, divorce, money and children issues are mainly heard at county court level, and therapists may be required to provide evidence or undertake assessments, therapeutic work or mediations to assist families in dispute. Recently, in cases where parents have intractable disputes about contact, the law has changed to allow the court to order participation in 'contact activities', which include mediation information and assessments, parenting information, and therapeutic domestic violence programmes (see s. 11, Children Act 1989, which came into force in December 2008). We have yet to see how the role of private therapists as providers of these activities will evolve in the context of these orders.

10.8 Dealing with requests for disclosure of client notes and records

Detailed information about responding to requests for disclosure of notes and records for court purposes can be found in *Therapists in Court* (Bond and Sandhu 2005). Information should be disclosed only where:

- the law requires (e.g. terrorism)
- the law permits, in the public interest (e.g. serious crimes, child protection, etc.)
- the client consents.

More recently, we wrote about making referrals and disclosure of information about clients, including capacity and consent, and discussion of specific situations where disclosure may be requested (see Bond and Mitchels 2008). If notes and records are regulated by the Data Protection Act 1998 and/or the Freedom of Information Act 2000, then clients may be entitled to access the information (see Bond and Mitchels 2008: Chapter 3).

When considering whether to disclose information, the checklists below provide a guide to thinking through the relevant issues.

Checklist: Issues to be considered in dilemmas over confidentiality

With all clients, including those who have refused consent, discuss with the client if appropriate, consider and ideally also discuss in supervision these issues:

- What is the likelihood of serious harm in this case?
- Is this serious harm imminent?
- If I refer, what is likely to happen?
- If I do not refer, what is likely to happen?
- Do the likely consequences of non-referral include any serious harm to the client or others?
- If so, are the likely consequences of non-referral preventable?

- What would have to happen to prevent serious harm to the client or others?
- Is there anything I (or anyone else) can do to assist in preventing this harm to my client or others?
- What steps would need to be taken to implement such assistance?
- How could the client be helped to accept assistance/the proposed action?
- Does my client have the mental capacity to give explicit informed consent (or refusal of consent) at this moment in time?
- If the client does not have mental capacity, then what are my professional responsibilities to the client and in the public interest?
- If the client has mental capacity but does not consent to my proposed action (e.g. referral to a GP), what would be my legal and professional situation if I went ahead and did it anyway?

(Bond and Mitchels 2008: 41)

Disclosure Checklist

It may help therapists in the decision-making process about sharing information to consider these points:

- Is this information regulated by the Data Protection Act 1998 (DPA) or the Freedom of Information Act 2000 (FOIA) (e.g. do the records comprise client-identifiable sensitive personal data held on computer or in a relevant filing system)?
- Were the notes made by a professional working for a public body in health, education or social care?
- What are the relevant rights of the person concerned under the Human Rights Act 1998 (HRA)?
- If working in the health community, is disclosure compliant with the Caldicott principles and guidance? See the Caldicott Guardian Manual (DH 2006) and the Glossary.
- Is there a legitimate requirement to share this information (e.g. statutory duty or a court order)?
- What is the purpose of sharing the information?
- If the information concerns a child, young person or vulnerable adult, is sharing it in their best interests?
- Is the information confidential? If so, do you have consent to share it?
- If consent is refused or there are good reasons not to seek consent, does the public interest necessitate sharing the information?
- Is the decision and rationale for sharing the information recorded?
- What is the most appropriate way to share this information?

(Bond and Mitchels 2008: 99)

When information is disclosed we recommend that the therapist makes a record of:

- date of disclosure
- what information was disclosed
- who the disclosure was made to
- how the disclosure was made (e.g. letter, phone call, etc.)
- whether the disclosure was with the client's consent
- if the disclosure was made without the client's consent, what was the reason for this.

10.8.1 Disclosure of documents for court proceedings in Scotland

You may be served with a court order called a 'Specification of Documents'. This can come from the Sheriff Court or the Court of Session. This is a court order which requires the disclosure of patient records for the purposes of litigation. This commonly arises in personal injury cases, for instance where a patient has become depressed as a result of a physical injury and is seeing a therapist to help them recover. Therapists practising in England may receive Scottish Specifications, for example if they are seeing a patient who lives in England but had an accident in Scotland and has raised proceedings there. If you receive a Specification, it is important that you do not provide any documents outside the scope of the order which the court has made. Specifications tend to be drafted in legalese and it will not always be clear what you have to provide. If you are in any doubt at all about what is required of you, then you should always contact a Scottish solicitor. The Law Society of Scotland keeps a list of all practising solicitors in Scotland. Further information is available at www.lawscot.org.uk.

10.9 Giving evidence in court

For full discussion of all matters relating to giving evidence, please see *The Therapist in Court* (Bond and Sandhu 2005). Below are some brief illustrations of court practice and etiquette, which may prove useful.

10.9.1 How do I address a magistrate or judge?

Magistrates may be lay people who 'sit' in court with a legally trained court clerk, or there may be a single, legally trained District Judge (formerly known as a stipendiary magistrate) who sits in the magistrates' court alone. Magistrates and District Judges should be called 'Sir' or 'Madam'. Police often still call them 'Your Worship' as a matter of tradition.

County courts also have District Judges who sit in 'chambers' (rather than in open court) and deal with the less serious matters and administrative hearings. They are addressed as 'Your Honour' and High Court and Court of Appeal judges are 'My Lord' or 'My Lady' (lawyers often pronounce it as m'lud or m'lady). Lawyers usually refer to each other in court as 'my learned friend' or by their name and role, e.g. 'John Smith, counsel for the defence'. Witnesses may refer to each other and/or to advocates by their names and roles, e.g. Professor Tim Bond, expert witness; or Barbara Mitchels, solicitor.

In Scotland you should always address a Sheriff in the Sheriff Court, or a judge in the Court of Session or High Court of Justiciary as 'My Lord' or 'My Lady'.

10.9.2 Giving evidence

The *Practice Direction: Family Proceedings: Experts [Family Division]* [2008] 1 WLR 1027 (referred to below as *Practice Direction: Experts 2008)* as came into force on 1 April 2008, and applies to all placement and adoption proceedings and the following family proceedings held in private:

- High Court's exercise of its jurisdiction in relation to children
- proceedings under the Children Act 1989 in any family court
- High Court and county court proceedings in relation to the maintenance or upbringing of a minor.

The practice direction can be found in full at www.hmcourts-service.gov.uk/cms/files/Experts-PD-flagB-final-version-14-01-08.pdf.

When therapists give evidence in any legal proceedings they may be regarded as an 'expert witness' or they may be an ordinary witness of fact. In family cases, the leave of the court is required before an expert witness is instructed, and the court will decide whether a therapist is to be treated as an expert in a particular case. Expert witnesses have special privileges – they are usually provided with all the documents in the case and they are allowed to sit in the court and hear the case as it progresses in order to evaluate the evidence they hear and, if necessary, advise the court. Witnesses of fact must remain outside the courtroom until they are called in. Experts are also usually paid by one or more of the parties to attend court. The overriding duty of an expert witness is to the court and not to the party who instructed them to attend. Reports of expert witnesses in family cases must follow the *Practice Direction (Experts) 2008.* In other types of case, experts are usually instructed by solicitors who will advise on form and procedure.

In Scotland, expert reports are prepared on a different basis. Jointly instructed experts are extremely rare, and typically each side in a litigation will have engaged their own experts. However, your duty as an expert is to the court and not to the side which has engaged you. The general rule in Scotland is that any witness who will be giving evidence in a case should not sit in on any of the other evidence until they have finished giving their own evidence. If you choose to sit in after your evidence has been concluded to hear the rest of the case, you should be aware that this may cause a difficulty if for some reason you are recalled to give further evidence later on. There may be situations in which it would be helpful to you and to the court for you to sit in on evidence of fact which will relate to the matters upon which you will be providing your expert opinion. In that situation, the lawyer instructed for the party that you are acting as expert for will make an application to the court for you to be allowed to sit in for the evidence of other witnesses. The other side have the right to object to this. You will not usually be allowed to sit in while the other side's experts give their evidence.

No matter what the status of the witness, certain guidelines are helpful:

- *Do not go beyond the remit of your expertise.*
  Experts should never go beyond the remit of their instructions or their expertise. Never agree to give expert evidence on a matter in which you do not have experience and expertise. There have been cases in which, regrettably, this has happened, to the detriment of a party, the child, justice, or possibly all three. The Court of Appeal gave helpful guidance for experts and lawyers in *R v Cannings* [2004] EWCA Crim 1, [2004] 1 WLR 2607.
- *Agree the fees, who is to pay and when payment is to be made first.*
  Always discuss fees and expenses with the party who is requesting your attendance. In family cases, there are rules and guidance about payment protocols (see the *Public Law Outline (2008)* and the *Practice Direction (Experts) 2008*). In other cases, the court rules may assist, but instruction and payment is a matter of contract between the parties and the witness. In criminal cases, instructions come from the Crown Prosecution Service or the defence lawyers. In civil cases, it will be one of the parties. If the party instructing you has public funding, they will need to get 'prior authority' from the Legal Services Commission to instruct you. If the matter is private, then the solicitor instructing you should also be responsible for agreeing and organising payment.
- *Ask for clear instructions in writing.*
  Always ask for a letter of instruction setting out the agreed terms of the instruction.

10.9.3 Preparation and court etiquette

Preparing for court

- Put all notes on to a treasury tag or, if using a ring binder, make absolutely sure that it will not ping open unexpectedly and spill all the notes in a muddle on the floor.
- Make sure that all notes are there, including original scribbled notes and any neat copies made later.
- Organise notes so you can find your way around them easily.
- Read through notes and any other material so that it is fresh in your mind.
- In Scotland, you will usually only be allowed to refer to documents while giving evidence if the documents in question have been lodged in court as 'productions'. The solicitor instructing you will usually have lodged your report as a production, together with any supplementary reports you may have produced. The reports prepared by experts instructed by the other side will also usually be lodged and you may be referred to these for your comments during the course of your evidence. If you think you will need to refer to a document, for instance your own clinical notes, you should discuss this with your instructing solicitor well in advance of the case coming to court to ensure that you will be able to access any documents you need while you are in the witness box.

At the courthouse

Always arrive in good time. All cases are listed on a notice board, which will tell you which court you are in. Some cases are listed by number only. If you don't know the number, find a court 'usher', a 'macer' in Scotland (usually a person in a black gown with a clipboard, whose role is to make cases run smoothly by getting the right people and things into the right places at the right time). The usher will need to know your name and role so that they are aware that you have arrived. Tell the usher where you are, if you are waiting to be called to give evidence and need to nip off to the lavatory or to the canteen.

Find the solicitor instructing you (with the usher's or macer's help if necessary) and make contact. They will then guide you as to what is expected. If there is no solicitor, ask the usher.

Do not discuss the case at all outside court with anyone except the solicitor instructing you or with their approval.

Before going into court, three things to remember:

- Visit the lavatory first if necessary – nerves may affect the bladder and you do not want to have to ask for a 'short break' soon after getting into the witness box!
- Turn off your mobile phone or pager.
- Leave any unnecessary clutter in the car and ensure that any parking ticket or meter covers the whole of the time you expect to be at court, or at least until lunchtime, when you can feed it again.

If a witness of fact, wait outside to be called in. If you are an expert witness, with the court's permission, go into court and sit near to the solicitor or party instructing you.

In court

Try not to come to court laden with unnecessary coats, bags and paraphernalia. Before you go into the witness box, find a place inside the courtroom to put everything (except notes and reading glasses) down first. Muddle in the witness box looks unprofessional.

Decide beforehand whether you will take the oath or affirm. The usher will ask when you go into the witness box.

Speak clearly and assertively. Take time to answer questions if necessary. If a question is unclear, seek clarification. When answering questions, turn your body slightly and address the answers directly to the magistrates or the judge. Turn back to the advocate for the next question. This makes it more difficult for advocates to interrupt. However, if interrupted in the middle of giving an answer, politely but firmly say that you will continue to answer the first question, then address the next one. Remember that the duty to the court is to 'tell … the whole truth and nothing but the truth'.

The best and most important advice is to have confidence and remember that you are the therapist and therefore a professional with expertise in your own field. The court will not have the level of understanding that you have of your work. Be prepared to explain professional issues to the court. If you can explain your actions, the content of your notes and your views to the court, and justify them professionally, then there is nothing to fear from questions from a judge or advocates in cross-examination.

Whilst giving your evidence, if you have a break (e.g. over the lunch hour), you should not discuss the case at all during that period. You should not go for lunch (or have any discussions even about other matters), with your instructing solicitor or client. This will avoid any suggestion that you may have acted improperly.

11 Professional Diligence for Therapists

I have heard that therapists can be reported to trading standards officers and that this can result in being prosecuted. Is this true?

I want to do more than the legal minimum. Am I creating liability for myself?

As a conscientious therapist, I want to do my best for my clients. What does the law require me to take into consideration to demonstrate professional diligence in serving my clients?

To be diligent is to provide careful and persistent work or effort. In this chapter we will consider what a member of the public should expect of a diligent therapist and what someone who is committed to providing therapy in a diligent manner ought to be considering. There are two levels of concern over professional diligence. The first is the use of the term in civil and criminal law to encourage and, when appropriate, enforce fair and honest business practice by creating offences punishable by fine or imprisonment. In this respect, the law is reasonably precise and well defined following the biggest revision of consumer protection regulations in 40 years. We will consider these legal developments first. However, there is a wider use of 'professional diligence' that is concerned with moral or ethical obligations which are over and above avoidance of legal liability. What ought a conscientious therapist take into consideration to demonstrate diligence in serving her clients? We will conclude with this question as a way of drawing the different themes of this book together.

11.1 Professional diligence and consumer protection

The legal use of the term 'professional diligence' refers to the basic requirements of people offering goods or services to others in the course of trade, and this includes professionals. The legal applications of 'professional diligence' are therefore directly relevant to therapists. The Consumer Protection from Unfair Trading Regulations 2008 apply in England, Wales, Scotland and Northern Ireland and are the implementation of a European Directive intended to standardise fair trading across countries. However, there are differences between countries across Europe and within the British Isles. These regulations introduce a substantially different approach to consumer protection guided by principles rather than prescriptive law. They are directed at business behaviour rather than the quality of the product.

Key concepts in these regulations are 'professional diligence', 'materially distorts' and the economic behaviour of the 'average consumer'.

Professional diligence is defined in the regulations as:

> The standard of special skill and care which a trader may reasonably be expected to exercise towards consumers which is commensurate with either (a) honest market practice in the trader's field of activity, or (b) the general principle of faith in the trader's field of activity. (Regulation 2)

A 'trader' is:

> Any person who in relation to a commercial practice is acting for purposes relating to his business, and anyone acting in the name or on behalf of a trader.

This widens the legal responsibilities beyond the therapist to any employees working with the therapist, such as receptionists, secretaries or trainees. It includes anyone who acts on behalf of or under the name of the therapeutic practice. In such circumstances, the reputation of the therapist for fair trading is at risk if any staff behaviour falls below the required standards. Professional diligence requires a standard of skill and care commensurate with honest market practice and acting in good faith within the particular line of business.

The aim of the legislation is to protect the fairness and integrity of any transaction on behalf of consumers and by protecting their opportunity to make an informed decision without any 'material distortion'. 'Material distortions' are ones that impair the consumer's ability to make an informed choice, leading them to make a decision or choice, that they would not have made otherwise. Underpinning the regulations are ideas about the 'average consumer' and whether or not the behaviour of the 'average consumer' would be distorted.

The European Court of Justice has offered guidance on who is the 'average consumer'. The 'average consumer' is 'reasonably well informed and reasonably observant and circumspect, taking into account social cultural and linguistic factors'. If commercial practice is likely to distort the economic behaviour of a clearly identifiable group, the average member of that group would be regarded as the 'average consumer'. If the members of a group who are particularly vulnerable because of their mental or physical infirmity, age or credulity, in a way which the trader could reasonably be expected to foresee, the trader, which includes members of professions, ought to have taken account of these characteristics. This is particularly relevant to therapists because of the potential vulnerability of clients.

The focus on practice and behaviour is particularly apparent in what this legislation prohibits. A commercial practice is considered unfair if it involves one or more of the following:

(a) Misleading action – where untruthful information is provided to consumers or information is presented in a way that deceives or is likely to deceive. Information may be considered deceptive even if it is factually correct, but has been used in ways that create a false impression.

(b) Misleading omission – where material information is omitted, hidden or provided in a manner that is unclear, unintelligible, untimely or ambiguous.

(c) Aggressive – if it impairs the consumer's freedom of choice or conduct through the use of harassment, coercion or undue influence. This includes exploiting a position of power in relation to the customer in ways that apply pressure.

The regulations specifically prohibit 31 different actions that may arise in the commercial world as ways of unduly influencing the economic behaviour of customers. Many of the behaviours that are prohibited in Schedule 1 relate to familiar ruses played on the unwary, such as prize money scams, luring people by promising bargains that are not really available in order to switch the customer to a more profitable product, or harassment by door-to-door salespeople to secure a sale. A listed behaviour is regarded as wrong in all circumstances and is therefore easier to enforce without being required to demonstrate the impact on an average consumer. The prohibition that is most directly relevant to therapists states: 'Falsely claiming that a product is able to cure illnesses, dysfunction or malformations is expressly prohibited' (Schedule 1, s. 17). A 'product' includes the provision of services. There are other ways in which a therapist could breach the levels of honesty and integrity that are expected by this legislation. It would be a misleading action if the therapist were to falsely claim membership of a professional body, claim false qualifications or experience, or to claim a fictitious endorsement of the therapy provided. It could be a misleading omission to omit known potential risks to the client in the proposed therapy. It could be regarded as aggressive for a therapist to pressurise a client to accept a particular type of therapy offered by putting sustained pressure on that client, especially if the client is vulnerable.

Enforcement in the UK (excluding Scotland) is undertaken by officers responsible for trading standards in local authorities and through the Office of Fair Trading. They may bring court actions in either the civil or criminal courts. In Scotland, prosecutions are usually conducted by the Crown Office and Procurator Fiscal Service on behalf of the Lord Advocate. These regulations do not currently entitle the consumer to sue or prosecute a trader directly in the UK. In contrast, a consumer in Ireland may seek an order directly from the courts or enlist the support of the National Consumer Agency to do so. This includes a right to compensation. The time limit in the UK for bringing a prosecution is either three years from the commission of the offence or one year after the discovery of the offence by the prosecutor.

The new legislation gives considerable powers of investigation by the relevant authorities. For further guidance, search for 'consumer protection regulations' in any of the major search engines and check that the guidance covers your country or region as there are local differences.

11.2 Doing more than the legal minimum

Most therapists are concerned to do more than simply provide their clients with the legal minimum out of their sense of personal commitment to their profession and a concern for the well-being of clients. Ethical guidance from professional bodies such as the British Association or Counselling and Psychotherapy (BACP) sets professional standards that are consistent with legal requirements but higher than the legal minimum requirements for professional diligence. These higher standards reflect a collective consensus within a professional body about what is required to provide clients with a reasonable level of service. Some individual therapists may adopt even higher standards than those characteristic of their profession out of personal commitment or to gain a market advantage over competitors. To what extent do these higher standards create any legal liability?

There is no simple answer to this question. Professional codes and frameworks inform disciplinary procedures within the profession. They open up a potential way for clients wanting to pursue any concerns through the use of professional conduct procedures, which may lead to the therapist being disciplined or, in the most serious cases, expelled from membership of that body. In cases where a therapist is being sued for negligence (see Chapter 3) the court will usually consult relevant professional codes and ethical guidance to inform them about what constitutes a reasonable standard of care and whether that standard has been breached. However, codes and guidance are persuasive but not binding on a court. The court may consider any professional requirements over and above professional diligence irrelevant or inappropriate in the circumstances of a specific case. Typically, one side in a tort action might be arguing for a higher standard than the other, and before reaching a decision the court may use a number of sources for guidance, including the opinions of expert witnesses.

Another way in which higher standards might create legal liability would be if the standards are incorporated into a legally binding contract. Doing so would demonstrate the therapist's commitment and offer reassurance to clients. In some circumstances the commitment to higher standards might earn a premium fee. For example, if a therapeutic practice offers therapists with particular qualifications or specified experience which is in short supply, it would be a breach of contract to substitute therapists with lower standing without the explicit agreement of the client.

Breach of a contractual term may entitle a client to make a legal claim for damages or some other remedy. The contents of codes and ethical frameworks do not automatically become terms of the therapeutic contract unless they are explicitly incorporated into the agreement by the therapist. For example, a contractual term might state:

Therapy will be provided in accordance with the current ethical codes/framework of ... [named professional body].

If and when statutory regulation is introduced, this will expand the potential ways for clients to raise concerns about a therapist which might lead to the removal of the therapist from the register and thus prevent that therapist from working under a specified regulated title. It will not curtail or remove any of those potential sources of legal action against a therapist already mentioned.

11.3 The benefits of following the law

In this book we have provided an overview of the areas of law currently considered essential to the practice of therapists. We have attempted to be as user-friendly and relevant to practice as possible. Sometimes we have been asked 'Why bother with the law?' That question may reflect a desire to remain within the informality and experimental nature of therapy characteristic of the 1960s and 1970s. More likely, the question implies a concern that focusing on law distracts from the quality of the relationship between the therapist and client, which can be so therapeutically powerful. Our response to both these positions is much the same. The world has moved on in ways that change the expectations of professional providers of services and in protecting the rights of clients. This is reflected in the social and legal context in which therapy is provided. In our view, the wise therapist can use legal requirements and provisions to add to the security of the work offered to the client. Used carefully, the law usually adds to the sense of containment and protection offered in therapy and protects against unexpected liability without constraining the therapeutic work. Working in ignorance of the law or without taking the law into account can undermine the therapeutic relationship and destabilise the work. The risk of blindly drifting into liability is greatly increased, often to the detriment of all parties. Observance of the law in routine practice usually roots therapeutic work in social structures that support the functioning of society in ways that protect the rights of all parties, especially clients and their service providers, and offers remedies when things go wrong. In our view, there is a considerable difference between using the law creatively and constructively to support a good therapeutic environment and becoming over-defensive or paranoid about the legal requirements to the detriment of the work. People who are very competent and well-respected therapists sometimes fail to appreciate the difference between a constructive and defensive approach to law because the law is outside their area of expertise and thus draws them away from their comfort zone. By writing this book we hope to redress the balance in favour of knowledge and an ability to make a realistic and constructive use of the resources that the law offers to therapy. Awareness, coupled with thoughtful and careful application of the law, is characteristic of mature practitioners and a profession willing to take their place in society.

List of Cases, Practice Directions, Judicial Guidance, Statutes, Statutory Instruments and EEC Directives and Regulations

Cases

Attridge Law v *Coleman* [2007] ICR 654. [2007] IRLR 88
Bolam v *Friern Hospital Management Committee* [1957] 2 All ER 118, [1975] 1 WLR 582
Bolitho v *City of Hackney Health Authority* [1997] AC 232. [1997] 4 All ER 771
Brock v *Wyner* [2001] 1 WLR 1159, 2 cr App R 745
Davies v *LHIM* (1983) 335 NW 2d 481 Michigan Supreme Court
Doe v *Roe and Roe* [1997]; 400 NY p2d 668
Dunlop v *Selfridge* [1915] AC 847
Eastwood v *Kenvon* [1840] 11 Ad & El 438
Egdell and *Others* [1990] 2WLR 471
Gillick v *West Norfolk and Wisbech Area Health Authority and Another* [1986] 1 AC 1212: [1985] 3 All ER 402 (HL) [1986] 1 FLR 224: [1985] 1 All ER 533 (CA): [1985] 3 WLR 830
Gore v *Van der Lann* [1967] 2QB 31. [1967] All ER 360
Hedley Byrne & Co Ltd v *Heller & Partners Ltd* [1963] 3 WLR 101. [1964] AC 465
HIH v *Chase Manhattan* [2001] EWCA Civ 1250. 2 Lloyds Rep 483 at page 163. and [2003] UKHL 6 [2003] Lloyds Rep IR 230
Hornal v *Neugerger Products Ltd* [1957] 1 QB 247
Hunter v *Hanley* [1955] SC at 204
Joel v *Law Union & Crown Insurance* [1908] 2 KB 863 CA
Kelly v *DPP* [2002] EWHC Admin 1428 166 JP 621
Khorasandjian v *Bush* [1993] 3 WLR 476 (Court of Appeal)
Lampleigh v *Braithwait* [1615] Hob 105
Lau v *DPP* [2000] 1 FLr 799 DC
London Borough of Lewisham v *Malcolm* [2008] UKHL 43
Majrowski v *Guy's and St Thomas's NHS Trust* [2006] UKHL 34
Market Investigations Ltd v *Ministry of Social Security* [1969] 2QB 173
Mazza v *Huffaker* [1983] 300 SE2d 833 (NC)
McLoughlin v *O'Brain* [1983] 1 AC 410 at 431
Melhuish v *Redbridge Citizens Advice Bureau* [2005] IRLR 419, EAT
Nicholsen v *Han* [1968] 12 Mich. App. 35, 162 NW 2d 313
Pettenden [1988] 7 CQJ 220
Phelps v *Hillingdon London Borough Council* [2000] 3 W.L.R. 776
Pratt v *DPP* [2001] EWHC 483

R (B) v (1) *Dr SS* (2) *Dr G* (3) *Secretary of State for the Health Department* [*Admin. Ct.*] [2005] 1 MHLR 347

R (B) v *Ashworth Hospital Authority* [*HL*] [2005] 1 MHLR 47

R v *Cannings* [2004] EWCA Crim 1. [2004] 1 WLR 2607

R v *H* (Assault of Child: Reasonable Chastisement) [2001] EWCA Crim 1024; [2001] 2 FLR 431

R v *Instan* [1893] 1 QB 453

R v *Souter* [1971] 1 WLR 1187, 2 All ER 1151

R v *Thomas and Thompson* 63 Cr App R 65 (CA)

Re W [2008] EWCA Civ 538 [2008] All ER (D) 258 (May)

Roy v *Hartogs* [1975]: 366 NYS 297. 300–301

S v *DPP* [2008] EWHC (Admin) 438

Sidway v *Governors of Bethlem Royal Hospital* [1985] AC 871 at 897

Tarasoff v *Regents of the University of California* [1976] (Sup. Ct. Cal. [1976];) 551 P 2d 334

W v *Egdell* [1989] 1 All ER 1089: [1990] Ch 359: [1990] 1 All ER 835

W v *Egdell* [court of Appeal] [1990] 2 WLR 471

W v *Egdell and others* [1990] 2 WLR 471

Werner v *Landau* [1961] Time Law Reports 8 March 1961: Solicitors Journal (1961) 105. 1008

Practice Directions and Judicial Guidance

Practice Direction: (Family Proceedings: Experts) [Family Division] [2008] 1 WLR 1027

Practice Direction (Public Law Proceedings: Case Management) [Family Division] [2008] 1 WLR 1040

The Ministry of Justice: *The Public Law Outline: Guide to Case Management in Public Law Proceedings* (PLO) 13 February 2008. at www.justice.gov.uk/docs/public_law_outline.pdf

Statutes

Adults with Incapacity (Scotland) Act 2000
Adoption and Children Act 2002
Age of Legal Capacity (Scotland) Act 1991
Care Standards Act 2000
Children Act 1989
Children Act 2004
Children and Adoption Act 2006
Children (Scotland) Act 1995
Child Support Act 1991
Civil Partnership Act 2004
Companies Act 1985
Compensation Act 2006
Criminal Justice Act 2003
Criminal Justice and Court Services Act 2000
Data Protection Act 1998
Disability Discrimination Act 1995
Disability Discrimination Act 2005
Drug Trafficking Act 1994
Education Act 1949

Education Act 2002
Electronic Communications Act 2000
Employer's Liability (Compulsory Insurance) Act 1969
Employment Act 2002
Employment Act 2008
Employment Relations Act 1999
The Employment Tribunals Act 1996
Equal Pay Act 1970
Family Law Reform Act 1969
Family Law (Scotland) Act 2006
Freedom of Information Act 2000
Health Act 1999
Health and Safety at Work Act 1974
Human Rights Act 1998
Interpretation Act 1978
Late Payment of Commercial Debts (Interest) Act 1998
Law of Property Act 1925
Law of Property (Miscellaneous Provisions) Act 1989
Limitation Act 1980
Local Authority (Social Services) Act 1970
Magistrates' Courts Act 1980
Mental Capacity Act 2005
Mental Health Act 2007
Mental Health (Care and Treatment) (Scotland) Act 2003
Minors' Contracts Act 1987
Misrepresentation Act 1967
Misuse of Drugs Act 1971
Occupiers Liability Act 1957
Occupiers Liability Act 1984
Occupiers Liability (Northern Ireland) Act 1957
Police Act 1997
Prescription and Limitation (Scotland) Act 1973
Proceeds of Crime Act 2002
Protection of Vulnerable Groups (Scotland) Act 2007
Protection of Children Act 1999
Protection from Harassment Act 1997
Race Relations Act 1976
Redundancy Payments Act 1965
Rehabilitation of Offenders Act 1974
Requirements of Writing (Scotland) Act 1995
Safeguarding Vulnerable Groups Act 2006
Sale of Goods Act 1979
Sex Discrimination Act 1975
Sexual Offences Act 1956
Sexual Offences Act 2003
Supreme Court Act 1981
Terrorism Act 2000

Trade Descriptions Act 1968
Tribunals, Courts and Enforcement Act 2007
Unfair Contract Terms Act 1977

Statutory Instruments

Business Protection from Misleading Marketing Regulations 2008 (SI 2008/1276)
Children (Admissibility of Hearsay Evidence) Order 1993 (SI 1993/621)
Civil Procedure Rules 1998 (SI 1998/3132)
Civil Procedure (Amendment No. 2) Rules 2008 (SI 2008/3085)
Civil Procedure (Amendment No. 3) Rules 2008 (SI 2008/3327)
Consumer Protection from Unfair Trading Regulations 2008 (SI 2008/1277)
Control of Asbestos Regulations 2006 (SI 2006/2739)
Data Protection (Subjects Access Modification) (Education) Order 2000 (SI 2000/414)
Data Protection (Subjects Access Modification) (Health) Order 2000 (SI 2000/413)
Data Protection (Subjects Access Modification) (Social Work) Order 2000 (SI 2000/415)
Data Protection (Processing of Sensitive Personal Data) Order 2000 (SI 2000/417)
Electronic Commerce (EC Directive) Regulations 2002 (SI 2002/2013)
Electronic Signatures Regulations 2002 (SI 2002/318)
Employer's Liability (Compulsory Insurance) Regulations 1998 (SI 1998/2573)
Employment Act 2002 (Dispute Resolution) Regulations 2004 (SI 2004/752)
Employment Equality (Age) Regulations 2006 (SI 2006/1031)
Employment Equality (Religion or Belief) Regulations 2003 (SI 2003/1660)
Employment Equality (Sex Discrimination) Regulations 2005 (SI 2005/2467)
Employment Equality (Sexual Orientation) Regulations 2003 (SI 2003/1661)
Employment Equality (Sexual Orientation) Regulations 2003 (Amendment) Regulations 2004 (SI 2004/2519)
Insurance Companies (Amendment) Regulations 1992 (SI 1992/2890)
Maternity and Parental Leave, etc Regulations 1999 (SI 1999/3312)
Mental Capacity Act 2005 (Appropriate Body) (England) Regulations 2006 (SI 2006/2810)
Money Laundering Regulations 2007 (SI 2007/2157)
National Health Service (Clinical Negligence Scheme) Amendment (No.2) (SI 2006/3087)
Part-time Workers (Prevention of Less Favourable Treatment) Regulations 2000 (SI 2000/1551)
Parental Responsibility Agreement Regulations 1991 (SI 1991/1478)
Paternity and Adoption Leave Regulations 2002 (SI 2002/2788)
Police Act 1997 (Criminal Records) (Registration) Regulations 2006 (SI 2006/750)
Police Act 1997 (Criminal Records) (Registration) (Scotland) Regulations 2006 (SI 2006/97)
Regulatory Reform (Fire Safety) Order 2005 (SI 2005/1541)
The Safeguarding Vulnerable Groups Act 2006 (Commencement No. 1) Order (SI 2007/3545)
The Safeguarding Vulnerable Groups (Northern Ireland) order (SI 2007/1351)
The Safeguarding Vulnerable Groups Act 2006 (Barred List Prescribed Information) Regulations (SI 2008/16)
The Safeguarding Vulnerable Groups Act 2006 (Transitional Provisions) Order 2008 (SI 2008/473)
The Safeguarding Vulnerable Groups Act 2006 (Barring Procedure) Regulations 2008 (SI 2008/474)

The Safeguarding Vulnerable Groups Act 2006 (Commencement No. 1) (Northern Ireland) Order 2008 (SI 2008/930 C. 45)

The Safeguarding Vulnerable Groups Act 2006 (Prescribed Criteria) (Transitional provisions) Regulations 2008 (SI 2008/062)

The Safeguarding Vulnerable Groups Act 2006 (Transitory Provisions) Order 2009 (SI 2009/12)

The Safeguarding Vulnerable Groups Act 2006 (Prescribed Criteria and Miscellaneous Provisions) Regulations 2009 (SI 2009/37)

The Safeguarding Vulnerable Groups Act 2006 (Commencement No. 2) Order 2008 (SI 2008/1320)

The Safeguarding Vulnerable Groups Act 2006 (Commencement No.3) Order 2009 (SI 2009/39)

The Safeguarding Vulnerable Groups Act 2006 (Devolution Alignment) Order 2009 (SI 2009/265)

The Safeguarding Vulnerable Groups Act 2006 (Commencement No.4) Order 2009 (SI 2009/1503)

The Safeguarding Vulnerable Groups Act 2006 (Miscellaneous Provisions) Regulations 2009 (SI 2009/1548)

The Safeguarding Vulnerable Groups Act 2006 (Miscellaneous Provisions) Order 2009 (SI 2009/1797)

Unfair Terms in Consumer Contract Regulations 1999 (SI 1999/2083)

Working Time Regulations 1998 (SI 1998/1833)

Working Time (Amendment) Regulations 2001 (SI 2001/3256)

EEC Directives and Regulations

EEC Regulation (E13020)

Equal Treatment Directive (76/207/EEC)

Equal Opportunities Directive (2006/54/EC)

Useful Resources

This list is compiled from a variety of sources and offered as a service. Inclusion in this list does not mean than any particular organisation is recognised or recommended by the authors or BACP.

Access Northern Ireland

This is a central government organisation which provides criminal history information about anyone seeking paid or unpaid work in certain defined areas, including children and vulnerable adults.
Address: Brooklyn, 65 Knock Road, Belfast, BT5 6LE
Tel 02890 259100
Fax 02890 259186
www.accessni.gov.uk
Email accessni@ani.x.gsi.gov.uk

Advisory, Conciliation and Arbitration Service – ACAS

Provides up-to-date information, independent advice and training. Works with employers and employees to solve problems and improve performance.
Aims to improve organisations and working life through better employment relations.
Address: National Office, 286 Euston Road, London, NW1 3JJ
Helpline 08457 47 47 47
Minicom 0845 606 1600
Lines open: Monday to Friday 8am–6pm, Saturday 9am–1pm
www.acas.org.uk

BACP Information Service

Help with ethical dilemmas and practice issues for members of BACP and their clients.
Address: BACP House, 15 St John's Business Park, Lutterworth, LE17 4HB
Ethical Helpdesk 01455 883316
Lines open: Monday to Friday 8.45am–5pm
www.bacp.co.uk
Email bacp@bacp.co.uk

Children and Family Court Advisory Support Service (CAFCASS)

Works with children and families involved in proceedings in family courts and advises the courts on the child's best interests.

Address: 6th Floor, Sanctuary Buildings, Great Smith Street, London, SW1P 3BT
Tel 0844 353 3350
www.cafecass.gov.uk

Centre for Accessible Environments

An information and training body on the accessibility of the built environment for disabled people.
Tel 0207 840 0125
www.cae.org.uk

Children's Legal Service

An independent national charity concerned with law and policy affecting children and young people.

Address: University of Essex, Wivenhoe Park, Colchester, Essex, CO4 3SQ
www.childrenslegalcentre.com
Email ele@essex.ac.uk
Tel 01206 872 466
National Education Line via Community Legal advice 0845 345 4345
Young People Freephone 0800 783 2187
Child Law Advice via Community Legal Advice 0845 345 4345
All lines open: Monday to Friday 9am–5pm

Community Legal Service Direct

Free advice about benefits, tax credits, housing, employment, education or debt problems.
Free confidential legal advice 0845 345 4345
Lines open: Monday to Friday 9am–6.30pm/Saturday 9am–12.30pm
General enquiries 0800 085 6643
Lines open: Monday to Friday 9am–5pm
www.elsdirect.org.uk

Criminal Records Bureau (CRB)

Aims to help organisations make safer recruitment decisions by providing wider access to criminal record information.
Address: CRB Services, PO Box 110, Liverpool, L69 3EF
General enquiries 0870 909 0811
Minicom 0870 909 0344
Lines open: Monday to Friday 8am–Saturday 10am–5pm
Welsh Language Line 0870 90 90 223
www.crb.gov.uk

Central Registered Body in Scotland (CRBS)

The CRBS was established by the Scottish Government, operated by Volunteer Development Scotland, which provides information and assistance upon request about the suitability of applicants for volunteer posts in Scotland, and free Disclosures (police checks) for volunteers in the voluntary sector working with children, young people and adults at risk in Scotland. Disclosures are obtained from **Disclosure Scotland** and the results passed on by CRBS to the individual concerned.

Address: Jubilee House, Forthside Way, Stirling, FK8 1QZ
Tel 01786 849777
Fax 01786 849767
Email info@crbs.ork.uk
www.crbs.org.uk

Crown Prosecution Service (CPS)

The Crown Prosecution Service handles police and other Crown prosecutions. It can provide general information between 9am and 5pm weekdays, answer-phone outside these hours. Can give practical advice but not legal advice.
Address: 50 Ludgate Hill, London, EC4M 7EX
Information Line 020 7796 8000
www.cps.gov.uk
Email enquiries@cps.gsi.gov.uk

Disclosure Scotland

Disclosure Scotland issues certificates – known as 'disclosures' which give details on an individual's criminal convictions, or state that they have none. Enhanced disclosures, where appropriate, will also contain information held by police forces and other government bodies.
Address: Disclosure Scotland, PO Box 50, Glasgow, G51 1YU
Telephone 0870 609 6006.
Lines open: Monday to Friday 8am–6pm
Fax 0870 609 6996
Email info@disclosurescotland.co.uk
www.disclosurescotland.co.uk

Equality and Human Rights Commission Disability Helpline

Provides advice and guidance to promote equality and human rights.
Textphone 0845 604 6610
Fax 08457 778 878
Scotland: Tel 0845 604 5510
The helpline is open Monday, Tuesday, Thursday and Friday 9am–5pm; Wednesday 8am–8pm.
Email info@equalityhumanrights.com

Her Majesty's Courts Service (HMCS)

HMCS provides administration and support for the Court of Appeal, the High Court, the Crown Court, the magistrates' courts, the county courts and the Probate Service.
Address: Customer Service Unit, Post l.40, 1st Floor 102 Petty France, London, SW1H 9AJ
Tel 0845 4568770
Fax 020 3334 4087
General website www.hmcourts-service.gov.uk/

See www.hmcourts-service.gov.uk/cmd/infoabout.htm for information about court proceedings and fees, and free, downloadable leaflets and forms providing guidance for parties.

Home Office

Address: Direct Communications Unit, 2 Marsham Street, London, SWIP 4DF
Tel 020 7035 4848
Lines open: Monday to Friday 9am–5pm
Minicorn 020 7035 4742
Lines open: Monday to Friday 9am–5pm
Email public.enquiries@homeoffice.gsi.gov
www.homeoffice.gov.uk

Insurers Specialising in Professional Liability Cover for Counsellors and Psychotherapists

H Balen & Co

Tel 01684 580771
Address: 2 Nimrod House, Sandy's Road, Malvern, Worcs. WRI4 1JJ
www.balen.co.uk
Email info@balens.co.uk

Devitt Insurance

Address: North House, St Edwards Way, Romford, Essex, RM1 3PP
Tell 01708 385917
www.devittinsurance.com
Email faith.mogan@churchhill.com

Harvey Pettitt & Partners

Address: Deerfold House, Deerfold, Salop, SY7 OEE
Tel 01568 770900
www.harverpettitt.uk.com
Email enquiries@harveypettitt.uk.com

Howden Insurance Brokers

Address: 1200, Century Way, Thorpe Park, Leeds, LS15 8ZA
Tel 0113 251 5011
www.howdenpro.com
Email enquiries@howdengroup.com

Towergate

Address: Airport West, Lancaster Way, Yeadon, LS19 7ZA
Tel 0113 391 9598 or 9555

www.towergateprofessionalrisks.co.uk
Email professionalrisks@towergate.co.uk

Independent Safeguarding Authority

The body responsible for implementing the Vetting and Barring procedures under the *Safeguarding Vulnerable Croups Act 2006*
Address: PO Box 181, Darlington, DL1 9FA
For making referrals under the statutory provisions (see Chapter 5 at 5.11) and for further information, general advice and help on the legislation contact ISA:
Address: PO Box 181, Darlington, DL1 9FA
Tel 0300 1231111
Lines open: between 8am and 5.30 pm Monday to Friday
Email info@vbs-info.org.uk
www.isa-gov.org.uk

Law Society

The Law Society is the professional body for solicitors which provides advice and practical help in finding a solicitor in your area, making complaints, news and other information about areas of law.
For further information about regulation and complaints about solicitors see the Solicitors Regulation Authority (SRA) below.
Search solicitors' firms from *Law Society* records:
www.lawsociety.org.uk/choosingandusing/findasolicitor.law
Address: The Law Society's Hall, 113 Chancery Lane, London, WC2A 1PL
Tel 20 7242 1222
Fax 020 7831 0344
Email contact@lawsociety.org.uk
www.lawsociety.org.uk

Legal Services Commission (LSC)

The LSC provides a national system of legal assistance and funding, The LSC regulates a quality control system including lawyers, mediators, Citizens Advice Bureaux and other advice providers. LSC funded advice is available about issues including: relationship breakdown, debt, housing, domestic violence, crime, benefits, asylum and immigration, education, employment, mental health and community care matters.

Address: 4 Abbey Orchard Street. London. SW1P 2BS
Helpline 0845 345 4345
www.legalservices.gov.uk
Email London@legalservices.gov.uk

National Register of Access Consultants

List of organisations providing information and assistance concerning disability access and facilities.
Address: 70 South Lambeth Road, London, SW8 1RL

Tel 0207 735 7845
Fax 0207 7840 5811
SMS 07921 700 089
Email info@nrac.org.uk
www.nrac.org.uk

National Society for the Prevention of Cruelty to Children – NSPCC

A free 24 hour service which provides counselling, information and advice to anyone concerned about a child at risk of abuse.
Address: Weston House, 42 Curtain Road, London, EC2A 3NH
24hr Helpline 0808 800 5000
Text phone 0800 056 0566
www.nspcc.org.uk
Email help@nspcc.org.uk
Cymru/Wales Helpline 0808 1002524
Textphone 0808 100 1033
Address: PO Box 62, Bangor LL57 4BN
Asian Helpline service in English 0800 096 7719
Asian helpline offers help in the following languages: Bengali/Sylheti, Gujurati, Hindi, Punjab, Urdu.
Lines open: Monday to Friday 11am–7pm
Email helpline@asian.nspcc.org.uk
Will endeavour to provide a translator service in other languages.

The Place2Be

Works inside schools to improve the emotional wellbeing of children, their families and the whole school community.

Address: 13/14 Angel Gate, 326 City Road, London, EC1V 2PT
Tel 020 7923 5500
www.theplace2be.org.uk
Email enquiries@theplace2be.org.uk

Solicitors Regulation Authority (SRA)

Address: Ipsley Court, Berrington Close, Redditch, B98 0TD
Professional Ethics helpline for solicitors (for advice on the Code of Conduct) 0870 606 2577 (inside the UK)
Lines open: 09.00 to 17.00. Monday to Friday.
Email professional.ethics@sra.org.uk
For complaints regarding solicitors, visit www.legalcomplaints.org.uk

Therapy Law

Legal website providing general information and guidance on law and ethics for therapists, with a regularly updated list of useful resources based on information from therapists and lawyers. Enquirers may also be provided on request with legal advice or help for specific problems, or facilitated to find local professional assistance where necessary.

www.therapylaw.co.uk
Email admin@therapylaw.co.uk

Trauma and Abuse Group – TAG

Provides information, support, training, encouragement and networking for counsellors, therapists, professional workers, carers and indeed anyone who is concerned or interested and any that are working with individuals who have suffered trauma and abuse.
Address: PO Box 3295. Swindon, SN2 9ED
www.tag-uk.net

Glossary

The Bar Council   Colloquial name for The General Council of the Bar which is the governing and regulatory body for barristers. It is a source of advice, information and can assist enquirers to find a barrister. See www.barcouncil.org.uk/

Burden of Proof   To secure a conviction in a criminal matter, the case for the prosecution has to be proved 'beyond reasonable doubt'. The burden of proof in civil cases is on the balance of probabilities, i.e. 'that it is more likely than not' that the events occurred (see Chapters 1 and 5).

Caldicott Guardians   People appointed to protect patient information in health and social care. They should be members of the management board or senior management team, senior professionals, or hold responsibility for promoting clinical governance within organisations providing health or social care. In 2006, the Department of Health produced the *Caldicott Guardian Manual* for their guidance, available from www.dh.gov.uk.

Caldicott Principles   Six principles for testing whether to disclose patient-identifiable information as part of recommendations on information sharing within the NHS and between NHS and non-NHS organisations. See the *Report on the Review of Patient-identifiable Information* by a committee chaired by Dame Fiona Caldicott in 1997 (the Caldicott Committee).

Client records   Generic term which includes all notes, records, memoranda, correspondence, photographs, artifacts and video or audio recordings relating to an identifiable client. Whether factual or process related, in whatever form they are kept.

Confidentiality   A wide ranging duty of managing information in ways that keep it secure and control its disclosure. It is concerned with protecting information that is identifiable with a specific person, typically because they are named, but the law will also protect the confidences of people whose identity can be deduced from the available information, perhaps because the listener knows some of the circumstances of the person being referred to. Thoroughly anonymised information in which the identity of specific people cannot be discerned is not protected by the law of confidentiality. A circle of confidentiality is a group of people sharing confidential information with the client consent, for example, a health care team, or a counselling organisation with group supervision.

Competent adult   A person aged over eighteen and mentally capable of giving valid consent.

Constitution Law   In the UK, the constitutional law consists of statute law (Acts of Parliament), subordinate legislation (Statutory Instruments) made under the authority of

Acts of Parliament, and case law (the decisions of the courts) in which the courts interpret and apply the statute law (see Chapter 1).

Contract Legally enforceable agreement, usually regulating the sale, lease or transfer of land, or the provision of goods, advice or services for an agreed price. In legal terms, the 'promisor' (or 'offeror') promises or offers to do something, in return for which the 'promisee' (or 'offeree') agrees to do or forbear from doing, or provide something in return (the 'consideration'). For example, a therapist may offer to provide therapy in return for which the client agrees to provide consideration in the form of payment, or a person may provide goods in return for the forgiveness of an outstanding debt (see Chapter 4).

The Criminal Records Bureau (CRB) An executive agency of the Home Office which maintains criminal records. Further information, including details of how to apply for disclosures, is available at: www.crb.gov.uk. In Scotland the Central Registered Body in Scotland (CRBS) (www.crbs.org.uk) provides access to disclosures for individuals working as volunteers in sensitive areas. Criminal records checks can be obtained from Disclosure Scotland (see www.discolourescotland.co.uk) and in Northern Ireland, from Access Northern Ireland (see www.accessni.gov.uk).

Crown Prosecution Service (CPS) Government department that advises the police on evidence and law, and prepares cases for prosecution. The CPS provides its own staff or agents as advocates in some cases, and instructs barristers (counsel for the prosecution) in other matters.

Disability/disabled Disability is defined in section 1(1) of the Disability Discrimination Act DDA 1995, subject to the provisions of schedule 1, as 'a person who has a physical or mental impairment that has a substantial and long-term adverse effect on his ability to carry out normal day-to-day activities'. The effect of an impairment is long term if it has lasted at least 12 months, or if it is likely to last at least that long, or for the rest of the person's life, or if it is likely to recur if in remission (DDA 1995, Sch 1. paras 2(1) and (2)). For further discussion of the Disability Discrimination Acts 1995 and 2005, with resources for information and help, see Chapter 7 at 7.1.and www.direct.gov.uk/en/DisabledPeople/ RightsAndObligations/DisabilityRights/DG_4001068. In the context of employment, see the *Disability Discrimination Act 1995 Code of Practice: Employment and Occupation* (the Code), issued on 1 October 2004, setting out the rights of disabled workers and duties of their employers, and see Chapter 9 at 9.6.1.

Duty of confidence A duty of confidence will arise whenever the party subject to the duty is in a situation where he either knows or ought to know that the other person can reasonably expect his privacy to be protected.

Forensic In general terms, forensic simply means court-related, i.e. a forensic report is one ordered by the court or prepared for use in court; forensic evidence is evidence used in court cases, etc.

Government In England, Scotland and Wales, the Queen is the Head of State, although in practice, the supreme authority of the Crown is carried by the government of the day.

The government comprises the Prime Minister (appointed by the Queen), the Ministers with departmental responsibilities, and those Ministers of State who form the Cabinet by the invitation of the Prime Minister. The legislature comprises the two Houses of Parliament – the House of Lords and the House of Commons (see Chapter 1).

Harassment   This can take various forms, depending on the context in which it happens. In the workplace, harassment may involve the violation of dignity or the creation of a hostile working environment. The Protection from Harassment Act 1997 was designed to protect victims of harassment, whatever form the harassment takes, wherever it occurs, and whatever its motivation. Breaches of the Protection from Harassment Act 1997 may constitute a criminal offence, or may give rise to civil liability, or both. See Chapter 9 at 9.7 for discussion of harassment in the workplace.

Judicial precedent   In case law, there is a hierarchy in judicial precedent, in which the decisions of the House of Lords bind every court below it (including the Court of Appeal) and the decisions of the Court of Appeal bind all lower courts. There are also constitutional conventions which have binding force but do not have statutory authority (see Chapter 1).

Judicial Studies Board   The purpose of the Judicial Studies Board (JSB) is to ensure that high quality training is delivered to enable those who discharge judicial functions in England and Wales to carry out their duties effectively, in a way which preserves judicial independence and supports public confidence in the justice system. For contact details see www.jsboard.co.uk.

Judiciary   The collective name for all judges, at all levels. The judiciary should be independent of government, and of politics, and are appointed from among experienced lawyers. Most of the present senior judges were formerly QCs, but the judiciary makes appointments from both branches of the profession. For further information see the Bar Council, Law Society and Judicial Studies Board websites.

The Law Society   Provides advice, information and guidance. The Law Society can assist enquirers to find a solicitor. For contact details see www.lawsociety.org.uk/ and Useful Resources.

Lawyer   The term 'lawyer' is very wide and includes judges. Queen's Counsel (QCs – senior barristers), barristers (members of the Bar), solicitors (solicitors of the Supreme Court), each Notary Public, and legal executives (legal personnel qualified in law who assist solicitors and the courts). In Scotland, the term lawyer includes attorney, solicitor and Sheriff.

List 99   This is a list that was maintained by the former Department for Employment and Skills (DfES), now the Department for Children, Schools and Families (DCSF). It is a confidential list of people whom the Secretary of State has directed may not be employed by local education authorities (LEAs), schools (including independent schools) or further education (FE) institutions as a teacher, or in work involving regular contact with children under 18 years of age. People who are convicted of one of a number of sexual or violent offences against a child under 16 years of age, or in some cases against an adult, are automatically deemed unsuitable to work with children and are included on List 99. Those subject to a court disqualification order are also included on List 99 automatically. List 99 may be integrated into the new lists created by the Vetting and Barring Scheme (see Chapter 5).

Multi Agency Public Protection Arrangements (MAPPA)   MAPPA provides a national framework in England and Wales for the assessment and managements of risk posed by serious and violent offenders, including individuals who are considered to pose a risk, or potential risk, of harm to children. The MAPPA framework will be integrated into the new Vetting and Barring Scheme (see Chapters 2 and 5).

Mental capacity   This is a legal concept, within which a person's ability to make rational, informed decisions is assessed (see the Mental Capacity Act 2005 and pp. 63–4). It is assumed in law that adults and children of 16 or over have the mental capacity and therefore the legal power to give or withhold consent in medical and health care matters. In Scotland, Section 1(1)(b) of the Age of Legal Capacity (Scotland) Act 1991 provides that a person of 16 years of age or over has legal capacity to enter into any transaction, which includes medical and health care matters. Section 2(1) provides that a person under the age of 16 can consent to a transaction of a kind commonly entered into by persons of his age and circumstances and on terms which are not unreasonable and Section 2(4) specifically provides that a person under the age of 16 years shall have the legal capacity to consent to any surgical, medical or dental procedure where, in the opinion of a qualified medical practitioner attending him, he is capable of understanding the nature and possible consequences of the procedure or treatment. These presumptions and rules are rebuttable, for example in the case of mental illness. A refusal of necessary medical treatment by young people over the age of sixteen but under eighteen may be overruled by the High Court (or Court of Session in Scotland). There is no one test for mental capacity to consent. Assessment of mental capacity is situation specific, and will depend upon the ability of the person to take in, understand and evaluate information including the risks and benefits of the decision to be made, and to communicate their wishes.

Negligence   The legal concept of negligence is based on the breach of appropriate professional standards and/or a duty of care, causing damage. In order to establish a case against a therapist, the plaintiff would have to prove:

- that a duty of care exists
- that the duty of care has been breached (i.e. conduct falling below the standards that the law demands)
- in the case of advice, that the defendant could have foreseen that any advice given would be relied upon (foreseeability)
- that, as a result of the action/omission complained of, the plaintiff suffered damage
- that the actions/omissions complained of were the cause of the damage.

(See Chapter 3).

Parental responsibility   The legal basis for decision making in respect of children under the age of eighteen, created by the Children Act 1989 and defined in section 3(1) as 'all the rights, duties, powers, responsibilities and authority which by law the parent of a child has in relation to a child and his property'. It is possible that the definition of parental responsibility may be further clarified in new legislation currently under consideration. More than one person can have parental responsibility for a child at the same time. It cannot be transferred or surrendered, but aspects of parental responsibilities can be delegated, CA 1989 s. 2(9), see Chapter 11 for further details. (For the equivalent provisions in Scotland, see Sections 1–3 of the Children (Scotland) Act 1995.)

Professional diligence Defined in the Consumer Protection from Unfair Trading Regulations 2008 as: 'The standard of special skill and care which a trader may reasonably be expected to exercise towards consumers which is commensurate with either (a) honest market practice in the trader's field of activity, or (b) the general principle of faith in the trader's field of activity' (Regulation 2).

Protection of Children Act (POCA) List The Protection of Children Act 1999 gave the Secretary of State power to keep a list of people who are unsuitable to work with children in childcare positions. Childcare organisations checked the list (and List 99) before employing someone in a childcare position. For details, see Chapter 12 of *Working Together to Safeguard Children* (DfES 2006C). Now superseded by the new Vetting and Barring Procedures, 'Child First' list, see Chapter 5 at 5.11.

Public interest The interests of the community as a whole, or a group within the community or individuals.

Restrictive covenant These are restrictions placed by agreement on the use of buildings and land, usually entered into for the benefit of neighbours and the community at the time that the land was sold or the building constructed, and they are set out in title deeds and leases. In titles that are registered with the Land Registry, restrictive covenants are entered on the register along with the title to the land, and a copy can be obtained for the payment of a fee from the local Land Registry (see Chapter 7).

Self-employed The distinction between self-employment and employment is not always easy to make (see the HM Revenue and Customs Booklet IR56/N139, *Employed or Self-employed?*) For help, ask local taxation offices, or look at the publications on the following website: www.hmrc.gov uk/selfemployed/tmaemployed or self-employed.shtml. (See Chapter 8 and Chapter 9 at 9.1.)

Sex Offenders Register Notification under Part 2 of the Sexual Offences Act 2003 (known as the Sex Offenders Register) is an automatic requirement on offenders who receive a conviction or caution for certain sexual offences. The notification requirements are intended to ensure that the police are informed of the whereabouts of offenders in the community. All offenders must reconfirm their details at least once every 12 months, and notify the police seven days in advance of any travel overseas for a period of three days or more. Failure to comply with these requirements is a criminal offence, with a maximum penalty of five years imprisonment (see Chapter 2).

Soft law Soft law includes the codes of practice issued by government departments, recommendations from official reports, and protocols adopted by statutory services. This type of law has no legal status in the courts in the sense that courts are not obliged to follow it until such time as Parliament gives it full legal status.

Supervision In the psychoanalytic tradition and in most therapeutic approaches in the USA, supervision is seen as supporting trainees who, on completion of their training, may work unsupervised. In Britain there is a tradition of independent supervision which continues throughout the training and the working life of the therapist, in which the supervisor is regarded as an independent facilitator with a specific role to support and mentor professional practice.

Tipping off Section 39 of the Terrorism Act 2000 creates an offence, colloquially known as 'tipping off', which, in relation to the investigation of terrorist activities, means disclosure of anything likely to prejudice the investigation, or interference with material which is likely to prejudice the investigation. The courts take this seriously, and the current maximum penalty for tipping off is five years' imprisonment, a fine or both (see Chapter 5).

Tort The law of tort in England and Wales is the general law of civil liability (in Scotland, it is called 'delict'). The word 'tort' (colloquially meaning injustice) was probably imported into our law from old French, having evolved from the Medieval Latin 'tortum' derived from *torquēre* (to twist) and 'tortus' (meaning twisted, crooked, dubious) (see Chapter 3).

Vetting and Barring Scheme (VBS) Set up by the Safeguarding Vulnerable Groups Act 2006, the Independent Safeguarding Board regulates activity with children and vulnerable adults. For details, and disscussion of the provisions in Wales, Scotland and Northern Ireland, see Chapter 5 at 5.11 (pp. 79–86).

Whistle blowing Colloquial term for giving information about bad practice by colleagues. Several professional organisations have published guidance on 'whistle-blowing' procedures, for example, the General Medical Council (GMC 2006: 43–5) and the British Psychological Society, *Professional Practice Guidelines for Counselling Psychologists* (BPS INF75/01/05) (BPS 2009).

References and Further Reading

Advertising Standards Authority (ASA) (2009) *British Code of Advertising. Sales Promotion and Direct Marketing* (11th edn). London: ASA. Available free at: www.asa.org.uk/asa/codes/ and from the Committee of Advertising Practice at www.cap.org.uk.

Anthony, K. (2007) *Introduction to Online Counselling and Psychotherapy*. BACP Information Sheet P6. Lutterworth: British Association for Counselling and Psychotherapy.

BACP (2004) *What is Supervision?* Lutterworth. British Association for Counselling and Psychotherapy.

BACP (2010) *Ethical Framework for Good Practice in Counselling and Psychotherapy*. Lutterworth: British Association for Counselling and Psychotherapy.

Bamber, L. et al. (eds) (2008) *Tolley's Health and Safely at Work Handbook*. London: Lexis Nexis/Tolley.

Bauer, J., Hafner, S. et al. (2003) 'The burn-out syndrome and restoring mental health at the working place', *Psychother Psychosom Med Psychol* 53(5): 213–22.

Bond, T. (1990) 'Counselling supervision – ethical issues', *Counselling, Journal of the British Association for Counselling* 1(2): 43–6.

Bond, T. (2009) *Standards and Ethics for Counselling in Action* (3rd edn). London: Sage.

Bond, T. and Sandhu, A. (2005) *Therapists in Court: Providing Evidence and Supporting Witnesses*. London: Sage.

Bond, T. and Jenkins, P. (2008) *Access to Records*. BACP Information Sheet GI. Lutterworth: British Association for Counselling and Psychotherapy.

Bond, T. and Mitchels, B. (2008) *Confidentiality and Record Keeping in Counselling and Psychotherapy*. London: Sage and British Association for Counselling and Psychotherapy.

Bond, T., Brewer, W. and Mitchels, B. (2008) *Breaches in Confidentiality*. BACP Information Sheet G2: Lutterworth: British Association for Counselling and Psychotherapy.

Bradgate, R. (2007) 'Formation of contracts', in M. Furmiston (ed.), *The Law of Contract*. London: LexisNexis Butterworths.

British Property Federation and the British Council of Offices (2002) *Code of Practice for Commercial Leases*. Available at: www.commercialleasecodeew.co.uk.

British Property Federation and the British Council of Offices (2004) *Renewing and Ending Business Leases: A Guide for Tenants and Landlords*. Available at: www.communities.gov.uk/publications/citiesandregions/renewingending.

British Property Federation and the British Council of Offices (2007a) *Guidance as to 'Model Clauses'*. Available at: www.bpf.org.uk/publications.

British Property Federation and the British Council of Offices (2007b) *Code for Leasing Business Premises in England and Wales*. Available at: www.leasingbusinesspremises.co.uk.

British Psychological Society (2009) *Professional Practice Guidelines for Counselling Psychologists*. Available at: www.bps.org.uk/publications/profpract/prof-pract_home.cfm (accessed 23/01/09).

Clark, J. (2002) *Freelance Counselling and Psychotherapy: Competition and Collaboration*. Hove: Brunner-Routledge.

Clark, M. (2007) 'Vitiating factors', in M. Furmiston (ed.), *The Law of Contract*. London: Lexis Nexis Butterworths.

Coates, M. (2004) *Guidance for Trainee Placements*. BACP Information Sheet T3. Lutterworth: British Association for Counselling and Psychotherapy.

Cohen, K. (1992) 'Some legal issues in counselling and psychotherapy', *British Journal of Guidance and Counselling* 20(1): 10–26.

Criminal Records Bureau (CRB) (2009) *Revised Code of Practice 2009*. London: CRBO.

Crown Prosecution Service (England and Wales) (2005) *The CPS: Provision of Therapy for Vulnerable or Intimidated Adult Witnesses Prior to a Criminal Trial – Practice Guidance*. London: Crown Prosecution Service. Also available at: www.cps.gov.uk.

Dale, H. (2008a) *Making the Contract for Counselling and Psychotherapy*. BACP Information Sheet P11. Lutterworth: British Association for Counselling and Psychotherapy.

Dale, H. (2008b) *Charging for Therapy in Private Practice: Pitfalls and Issues*. BACP Information Sheet P2. Lutterworth: British Association for Counselling and Psychotherapy.

Department of Trade and Industry (DTI): *Redundancy Payments* (URN 98/95). London: Department of Trade and Industry. *Offsetting Pensions Against Redundancy Payments* (RLP1). London: Department of Trade and Industry. *Time Off for Job Hunting when Facing Redundancy* (PL703). London: Department of Trade and Industry. All leaflets are available at: www.direct.gov.uk/en/Employment/RedundancyAndLeavingYourJob/Redundancy/DG 10026616

Note that the role of the former DfES is now part of the Department for Children, Schools and Families, see www.dcsf.uov.uk/. The DfES publications listed below may be ordered from TSO, or through the DCSF.

DfES (2004a) *Every Child Matters: Change for Children Programme* Ref: DfES/1081/2004 www.everychildmatters.gov.uk.

DfES (2004b) *Working with Voluntary and Community Organisations to Deliver Change for Children and Young People*.

DfES (2004c) *National Service Framework (NSF) for Children, Young People and Maternity Service*.

DfES (2004d) *Five Year Strategy for Children and Learners*.

DfES (2004e) *Every Child Matters: Change for Children in Schools*. Ref: DfES/1089/2004.

DfES (2004f) *Every Child Matters: Change for Children in the Criminal Justice System*. Ref: DfES/1092/2004.

DfES (2004g) *Every Child Matters: Change for Children in Health Services*. Ref: DoH/1091/2004.

DfES (2006a) *What to Do If You Are Worried That a Child is Being Abused*. Norwich: TSO.

DfES (2006b) *Information Sharing: A Practitioner's Guide*. Norwich: TSO.

DfES (2006c) *Working Together to Safeguard Children: A Guide to Inter-Agency Working to Safeguard and Promote the Welfare of Children*. Norwich: the Stationery Office. Available for download at www.everychildmatters.gov.uk/workingtogether and from TSO.

DH (2000) *Framework for Assessment of Children in Need and their Families*. Norwich: TSO.

DH (2003a) *Confidentiality: NHS Code of Practice*. London: Department of Health.

Disability Discrimination Act 1995 Code of Practice: Employment and Occupation. Issued on 1 October 2004. Norwich: TSO. See: www.tsoshop.co.uk. See also www.direct.gov.uk/en/DisabledPeople/RightsAndObligations/DisabilityRights/DG_4001068.

Disability Discrimination Act – Easy Read Guide; Disability Discrimination Act – BSL Video Guide; Discrimination Act – Braille Guide; Disability Discrimination Act – Audio Guide. London: The Stationery Office. All available from The Stationery Office (TSO) bookshop or online shop (www.tsoshop.co.uk).

Disability Rights Commission *Making Access to Goods and Services Easier for the Disabled: A Practical Guide for Small Business and Service Providers*. London: Equality and Human Rights Commission. Available at: www.directgov.uk/en/DisabledPeople/Everyday Lifeandaccess/Everydayaccess/DG_4018353.

Donaldson, Sir Liam (2003) *Making Amends*. NHS Consultation Paper. London: Department of Health. Available at: www.doh.gov.uk/makingamends.

Employment Rights: To download all the legislation and guidance as documents from the internet, see www.berr.gov.uk/whatwedo/employment/employmentlegislation/ employment-act-2008/index.html. To read the guidance to the Employment Act 2008, go to www.opsi.gov.uk/acts/acts2008/en/ukpgaen_20080024_en_1.htm.

Equal Opportunities Commission (2003) *Code of Practice on Equal Pay*. London: EOC. Available at www.equalityhumanrights.com/uploaded.../code_of_practice_equalpay.pdf.

Feldman, S. and Ward. T. (1979) 'Psychotherapeutic injury: reshaping the implied contract as an alternative to malpractice', *North Carolina Law Review* (58): 63–96.

Feltham, C. (1999) *Developing Counsellor Supervision*. London: Sage.

Furmston, M. (ed.) (2007) *The Law of Contract*. Butterworths Common Law Series. London: LexisNexis Butterworths.

Gabriel, L. and Casemore, R. (2008) *Practical Aspects of Setting up a Counselling Service*. BACP Information Sheet EI. Lutterworth: British Association for Counselling and Psychotherapy.

GMC (2004) *Confidentiality: Protecting and Providing Information*. London: General Medical Council. Also available at: www.gmc-uk.org/standards/default.htm.

GMC (2006) *Good Medical Practice*. London: General Medical Council. Also available at www.gmc-uk.org.

Hackney, H. and Goodyear, R. (1984) 'Carl Rogers' client-centered approach to supervision', in R. Levant and J. Shilen (eds), *Client Centered Therapy and the Person Centered Approach*. New York: Praeger.

Hawkins. P. and Shoet. R. (1996) *Supervision in the Helping Professions*. Milton Keynes: Open University Press.

Her Majesty's Courts Service (HMCS) publish a range of leaflets. These are available at www.hmcourts-service.gov.uk/
Making a claim? Some questions to ask yourself (Leaflet EX301)
How to make a claim (Leaflet EX302)
Debt recovery for businesses (Leaflet EX350)
Court Fees – do I have to pay them? (Leaflet EX 60A)
No reply to my claim form – what should I do? (Leaflet EX304)
The defendant disputes all or part of my claim (Leaflet EX306)
The defendant admits my claim – I claimed a fixed amount of money (Leaflet EX309)
The defendant admits my claim – I did not claim a fixed amount of money (Leaflet EX308)
The small claims track (Leaflet EX307)
The fast track and the multi track (Leaflet EX305)
A claim has been made against me – what should I do? (Leaflet EX303)
I have been asked to be a witness – what do I do? (Leaflet EX341)
Some things you should know about coming to a court hearing. (Leaflet EX342)
Money Claim On Line is also available at: www.hmcourts-service.gov.uk/onlineservices/ mcol/index.htm.

Home Office (1966) *Memorandum of Good Practice in Video Recorded Interviews with Child Witnesses in Criminal Proceedings*. London: Home Office. Available from The Stationery Office.

Home Office Circular 16/2005, *Guidance on Offences Against Children*. London: Home Office. Available from The Stationery Office.

HM Revenue and Customs: *Employment Status Indicator (ESI) Tool*. London: Inland Revenue. Available at www.hmrc.gov.uk/employment-stauts/index.htm.

HM Revenue and Customs *Thinking of Working for Yourself?* Booklet SE1. London: Inland Revenue. Available at www.hmrc.gov.uk/startingup/taxgate.htm.

HM Revenue and Customs *Employed or Self-Employed?* Leaflet IR56. London: Inland Revenue. Available at www.hmrc.gov.uk/pdfs/ir56.pdf.

HM Revenue and Customs *Giving Your Business the Best Start with Tax: Advice and Assistance on Business Start-up*. London: Inland Revenue. See www.hmrc.gov.uk/startingup/.

HM Revenue and Customs *Advice and Assistance on VAT Registration, How and Where to Register, and Accounting Schemes to Simplify VAT Accounting*. London: Inland Revenue. See www.hmrc.gov.uk/vat/index.htm?_nfpb=true&_pageVAT_Home

HM Revenue and Customs *Helpline for the Newly Self Employed* (Telephone 08459 15 45 15).

Hudson-Allez, G. (1997) *Time Limited Therapy in a General Practice Setting*. London: Sage.

Jackson, H. (2003) (updated by Denise Chaytor) *Personal Safety for Practitioners Working in High Risk Environments and with High Clients*. BACP Information Sheet G5. Lutterworth: British Association for Counselling and Psychotherapy.

Jacobs, M. (ed.) (1996) *In Search of Supervision*. Buckingham: Open University Press.

Jacobs, M. (2007) *Dual Roles*. BACP Information Sheet G3. Lutterworth: British Association for Counselling and Psychotherapy.

Jenkins, P. (2002) *Legal Issues in Counselling and Psychotherapy*. Ethics in Practice Series. London: Sage.

Jenkins, P. (2007) *Counselling, Psychotherapy and the Law*. London: Sage.

Jenkins, P. Keter. V. and Stone. J. (2004) *Psychotherapy and the Law: Questions and Answers for Counsellors and Therapists*. London: Whurr.

Kermani, E. (1989) *Handbook of Psychiatry and the Law*. London: Year Book Publishers.

Laming, Lord (2003) *The Victoria Climbié Inquiry: Report of an Inquiry by Lord Laming*. Norwich: TSO.

Mason, J. and Laurie, G. (eds) (2006) *Mason & McCall Smith's Law and Medical Ethics* (7th edn). Oxford: Oxford University Press.

Mearns, D. (2004a) *How Much Supervision Should You Have?* Lutterworth: British Association for Counselling and Psychotherapy.

Mearns, D. (2004b) (updated by Gabrielle Syme) *Counselling and Psychotherapy Workloads*. BACP Information Sheet G4. Lutterworth: British Association for Counselling and Psychotherapy.

Mitchels, B. (2009) 'Safeguarding vulnerable groups', *Therapy Today* 20(9): 26–30.

Moore, S. (2005) *Professional Aspects of Setting Up a Counselling Service*. BACP Information Sheet P1. Lutterworth: British Association for Counselling and Psychotherapy.

Oliphant, K. (2007) *The Law of Tort*. London: Butterworths.

Otto, R. and Schmidt, W. (1991) 'Malpractice in verbal psychotherapy: problems and some solutions'. *Forensic Reports* 4: 309–336.

Page, S. and Wosket, V. (1998) *Supervising the Counsellor*. London: Routledge.

Pearl, D. (2006) *Care Standards Legislation Handbook*. Bristol: Jordan Publishing.

Powers, M. and Harris, N. (eds) (2000) *Clinical Negligence* (3rd edn). London: Butterworths.

Proctor, B. (1986) 'Supervision: a co-operative exercise in accountability', in M. Marken and M. Payne (eds), *Enabling and Ensuring: Supervision in Practice*. Leicester: National Youth Bureau.

Rawlins, M. (2003) in *Medeconomics* November: 2.

The Scottish Executive (2003) *It's Everyone's Job to Make Sure I'm Alright: Report of the Child Protection Audit and Review*. Edinburgh: Scottish Executive. Available at www.scotland.gov.uk/library5/education/iaar.pdf.

The Scottish Executive (2004a) *Protecting Children and Young People: The Charter*. Edinburgh: Scottish Executive. Available at www.scotland.gov.uk/library5/edicatopm/ecel.pdf.

The Scottish Executive (2004b) *Protecting Children and Young People: The Framework for Standard*. Edinburgh: Scottish Executive. Available at www.scotland.gov.uk/about/ED/CnF/00017834/page142392928.pdf.

The Scottish Office (1998a) *Protecting Children: A Shared Reponsibility*. Guidance on Inter-Agency Co-operation. Available at www.scotland.gov.uk/Topics/People/Young-People/children-families/17834/14723.

The Scottish Office (1998b) *Protecting Children: A Shared Reponsibility*. Guidance for Health Professionals in Scotland. Available at www.scotland.gov.uk/Topics/People/Young-People/children-families/17834/14723.

Sills, C. (ed.) (2006) *Contracts in Counselling and Psychotherapy* (2nd edn). London: Sage.

Slade, E. (2008) *Tolley's Employment Handbook*. London: LexisNexis.

Tasker, B. (2008) *Assessment in Counselling and Psychotherapy*. BACP Information Sheet P13. Lutterworth: British Association for Counselling and Psychotherapy.

Trading Standards (2008) *Trading Standards Guidance on the Consumer Protection from Unfair Trading Regulations 2008*. Available at: www.tradingstandards.gov.uk/.

More detailed information is available through your local trading standards service website. To find your local service use the postcode search on the website above.

For personal help with a problem within the UK you can call Consumer Direct on 08454 040506 (minicorn users 08451 281384) or visit the Consumer Direct website at www.consurnerdirect.gov.uk.

If you are a UK consumer having a problem with a trader based in a difference European country the there is a special service offering advice and support, the UK European Consumer Centre (UK ECC) at www.ukecc.net, which is hosted by the Trading Standards Institute.

Turner, M. and Kennedy, M. (2008) *Tarasoff and the Duty to Warn Third Parties*. London: Department of Forensic Psychiatry, Institute of Psychiatry. Available at http://pb.rcpsych.org/cgi/reprint/21/8/465.pdf (accessed 26/11/09).

Williams, G.L. (1963) *Learning the Law*. London: Stevens & Sons.

Index

Research Methods Books from SAGE

DISCOVERING STATISTICS USING SPSS THIRD EDITION

ANDY FIELD

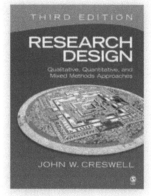

THIRD EDITION
RESEARCH DESIGN
Qualitative, Quantitative, and Mixed Methods Approaches

JOHN W. CRESWELL

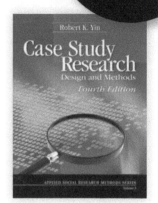

Robert K. Yin

Case Study Research
Design and Methods
Fourth Edition

APPLIED SOCIAL RESEARCH METHODS SERIES

Second Edition

QUALITATIVE INQUIRY & RESEARCH DESIGN
Choosing Among Five Approaches

John W. Creswell

Doing a Literature Review

Chris Hart

STATISTICS for People Who (Think They) HATE STATISTICS

3

NEIL J. SALKIND

SECOND EDITION

INTERVIEWS
Learning the Craft of Qualitative Research Interviewing

Steinar Kvale
Svend Brinkmann

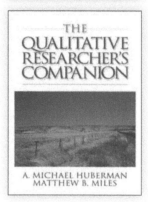

THE
QUALITATIVE RESEARCHER'S COMPANION

A. MICHAEL HUBERMAN
MATTHEW B. MILES

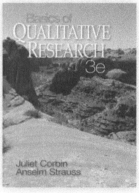

Basics of
QUALITATIVE RESEARCH
3e

Juliet Corbin
Anselm Strauss

www.sagepub.co.uk

SAGE